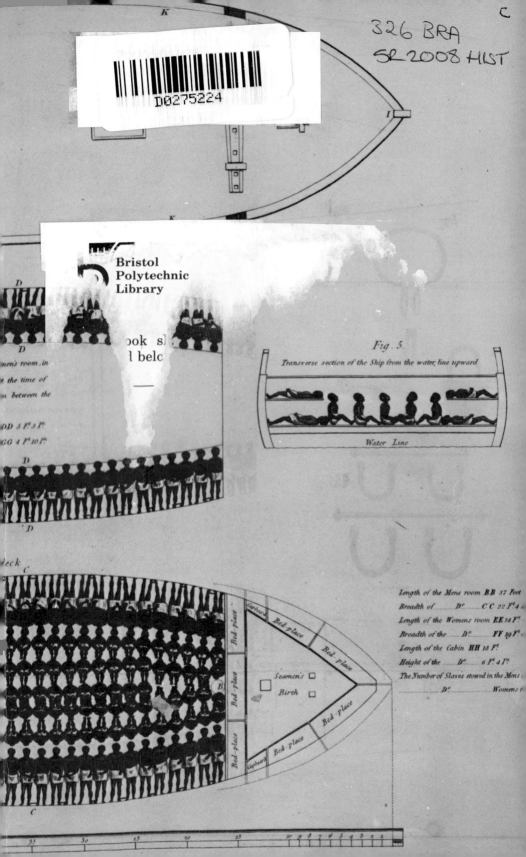

K

I

K

D

D

men's room, in

t the time of

n between the

DD 5 F. 3 I.
GG 4 F. 10 I.

D

D

ok sh
l belo

Fig. 5.

Transverse section of the Ship from the water line upward

Water Line

deck

B

Bed-place

Bed-place

Bed-place

Bed-place

Capstern

Capstern

Seamen's
Birth

Bed-place

Bed-place

Bed-place

Bed-place

C

C

Length of the Mens room BB 37 Feet
Breadth of ⸻ D° ⸻ CC 22 F. 4
Length of the Womens room EE 14 F.
Breadth of the ⸻ D° ⸻ FF 19 F.
Length of the Cabin HH 18 F.
Height of the ⸻ D° ⸻ 6 F. 4 I.
The Number of Slaves stowed in the Mens
⸻ D° ⸻ Womens

The Fight Against Slavery

Terence Brady and Evan Jones

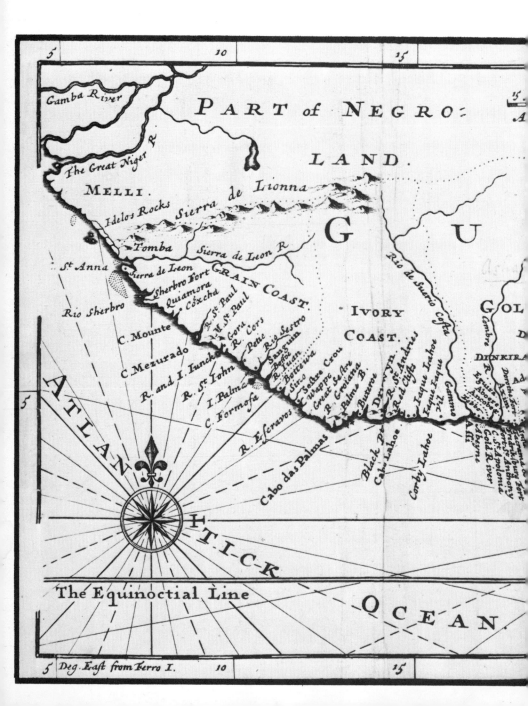

Published by the
British Broadcasting Corporation
35 Marylebone High Street
London W1M 4AA

ISBN: 0 563 12868 2
First published 1975

© Terence Brady and Evan Jones 1975

Picture research by Angela Murphy

Printed in Great Britain by
John Blackburn Ltd
Leeds, West Yorks

The Fight Against Slavery

British Broadcasting Corporation

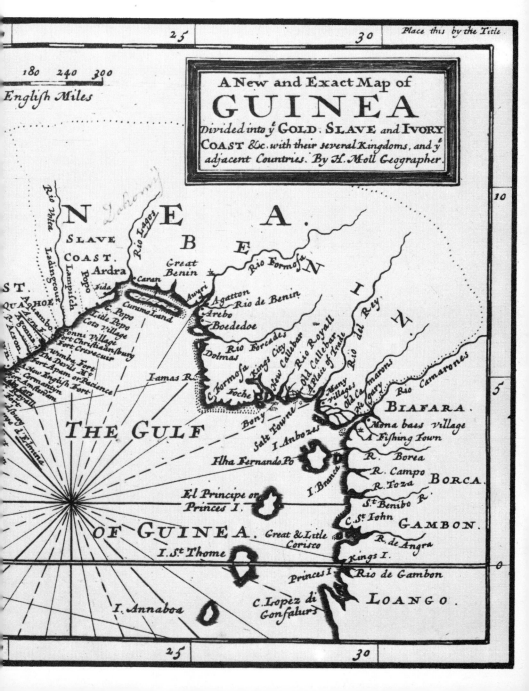

Place this by the Title

180 240 300
English Miles

A New and Exact Map of
GUINEA
Divided into y GOLD. SLAVE and IVORY
COAST &c. with their several Kingdoms, and y
adjacent Countries. By H. Moll Geographer.

Contents

The Wedgwood
medallion

This book is based on, and amplifies, the historical background of the
BBC/Time Life television series, *The Fight Against Slavery*, which was
written and narrated by Evan Jones, and produced and directed by
Christopher Ralling.

Documentary drama aims at the truth of art, if this can be achieved
without the distortion of known fact. To give historical events a
dramatic shape is primarily a matter of selection. Some things are
stressed, some omitted or combined. Actual locations may be used, or
reconstructed, or similar locations chosen. The words of the characters are quoted whenever possible, but sometimes of necessity invented.

This book follows the structure of the series, but aims at the more
conventional truth of history, which were it not hallowed by tradition
might be found to be similarly selective, partial or interpreted. We
hope that the viewer of the series and the reader of the book will find
that these truths are not dissimilar, and moreover that these recon-
siderations of the past help us to understand, and even to influence, the
present.   T.B.   E.J.

Introduction

The medallion of the anti-slavery movement was a cameo struck in 1786 by Josiah Wedgwood depicting a suppliant negro slave, and bearing the legend 'Am I Not A Man And A Brother?' While this appeal still finds echoes in our world today, in England in the 1700s it was perhaps even more heartfelt. Until a small and disparate group of people espoused their cause and devoted their lives and labours to fighting for their manumission, the kidnapped negro slaves were regarded both in law and by the vast majority of their captors and masters merely as property, and thus neither deserving of nor entitled to any human rights whatsoever. Thus a notorious captain of a slave ship could, and indeed did (the case of the *Zong*, 1781), jettison a large number of his living slave cargo into the sea when his safe return to land was threatened, perfectly secure in the knowledge that although the law might deem such an action cruel, it could certainly not find it improper.

Facts such as this, and other examples of the treatment accorded to captured Africans both in transit to the New World and in the plantations where they were subsequently enslaved, facts painstakingly researched, collected and made public by the abolitionists, created a violent public reaction. It became only a question of time before Parliament had to swallow its prejudices, ignore the powerful remonstrations of certain members with vested interests and bring in measures which finally brought to an end the most shaming chapter in the commercial, economic and social history of England.

Modern historical opinion has often inclined to the view that the slave trade was abolished more because of economic factors – namely the decline of the West Indies as a source of colonial wealth for Great Britain – rather than, as was earlier believed, by the massive growth of humanitarian awareness. Certainly Britain was busy patting herself on the back when she should have still been hanging her head in shame at having allowed such a fearful traffic to exist for such a long time, but even so it is only fair to say that the two influences which destroyed the slave trade, namely economics and philanthropy, were interdependent, and abolition would have taken considerably longer to achieve had not these two forces been at work simultaneously. Nor should much credence be given to the present way of thinking, which is inclined to undervalue the massive achievement of men such as William Wilberforce, Thomas Clarkson, Granville Sharp, James Stephen and Thomas Buxton, and which sees the abolitionists as indulgent dillettantes, who built exaggerated reputations on an already doomed and collapsing traffic. It can certainly be argued that these men's belief in the superiority of white Christian civilisation and the imposition of this ethic on the liberated negro later led to our high-handed colonial expansion and arrogant imperialism, but all these men were aware of at the time was the horrific immorality of the slave trade, and their only commitment was to its ultimate downfall and to the end of slavery. Certainly Britain subsequently hid behind this smokescreen of 'enlightened humanism' while subjugating any black people unwilling to accept the advances of Christian white civilisation. Even nowadays white superiority over black in certain countries is backed with religious justifications. But the men who were simply opposed to the barbarity of slavery and the immorality of the slave trade cannot be blamed for not being able to control future events, or judged by standards of which they were not aware.

They were only a small band of men, some rich, some poor, led by the frail and gentle William Wilberforce, and backed in Parliament by two political enemies, William Pitt the Younger and Charles James Fox, fighting to end a system that made England rich and prosperous, depopulated a continent and left wounds which are still unhealed today. At a time when there was no mass media to help them incite, educate or organise the population, when the might and wealth of the country stood arraigned against them and when Napoleon was threatening the very security of their homeland, they managed to conduct a campaign of mass protest and to end the trade that had stolen from the African continent what has been estimated at forty million men, women and children.

Now that the Americas are settled, it is permitted to deplore the destruction and dispossession of the American Indians. It must also be remembered that the settlement of America was accomplished by the destruction of West African civilisations, the Empire of Songhay, the Kingdom of Benin, the Hausa cities, the Empire of Kanem Bornu, Oyo, Yoruba, Asante, Denkyira, Mali and Mandingo. These also were nations with histories, languages, customs, rulers, assemblies, law, art and religion. In the days of slavery, and at the height of imperialism, it was convenient to forget this. It can be remembered now.

TO BE SOLD & LET

BY PUBLIC AUCTION,

On MONDAY the 18th of MAY, 1829,

UNDER THE TREES.

FOR SALE,

THE THREE FOLLOWING

SLAVES,

VIZ.

HANNIBAL, about 30 Years old, an excellent House Servant, of Good Character.
WILLIAM, about 35 Years old, a Labourer.
NANCY, an excellent House Servant and Nurse.
The MEN belonging to "LEECH'S" Estate, and the WOMAN to Mrs. D. SMIT

TO BE LET,

On the usual conditions of the Hirer finding them in Food, Clothing, and Medical Assistance,

THE FOLLOWING

MALE and FEMALE

SLAVES,

OF GOOD CHARACTERS.

ROBERT BAGLEY, about 20 Years old, a good House Servant.
WILLIAM BAGLEY, about 18 Years old, a Labourer.
JOHN ARMS, about 18 Years old.
JACK ANTONIA, about 40 Years old, a Labourer.
PHILIP, an Excellent Fisherman.
HARRY, about 27 Years old, a good House Servant.
LUCY, a Young Woman of good Character, used to House Work and the Nursery.
ELIZA, an Excellent Washerwoman.
CLARA, an Excellent Washerwoman.
FANNY, about 14 Years old, House Servant.
SARAH, about 14 Years old, House Servant.

Also for Sale, at Eleven o'Clock,

Fine Rice, Gram, Paddy, Books, Muslins, Needles, Pins, Ribbons, &c. &c.

AT ONE O'CLOCK, THAT CELEBRATED ENGLISH HORSE

BLUCHER,

ADDISON PRINTER GOVERNMENT OFFICE.

John Newton

REV.^d JOHN NEWTON

BORN 1725-DIED 1807

Sailors inspecting slaves before purchase

1. The Old African Blasphemer

'How sweet the name of Jesus sounds,
In a believer's ear!
It soothes his sorrows, heals his wounds,
And drives away his fears.'

This famous Anglican hymn, still sung in many churches around the world today, was the work of the captain of a slave ship who penned it while awaiting the arrival of a slave coffle (the term used for a gang of slaves chained together) on the coast of Guinea. The author was John Newton, an extraordinary character even in a century famous for its eccentrics. Newton was the son of a stern and authoritarian merchant sea captain. He was first sent to sea in his father's ship when only ten years old. Throughout his life he suffered from alternating bouts of deep religious fervour (he avowed to join the ministry half a dozen times before he was sixteen) and utter melancholia. As a young man and ordinary seaman he dedicated himself to a life of profanity and wild drunkenness, and was so notorious for his foul, blasphemous language that his fellow sailors frequently anticipated their ship to be wrecked by a vengeful deity as punishment for their shipmate's impiety. Even certain hardened sea captains under whom he served were only too happy to see the back of him when he deserted, which he frequently did.

Two events early on in his life helped to correct the dissolute Newton's ways. When he was sixteen he met and fell passionately in love with a thirteen-year-old girl called Mary Catlett. He compared their passion to that of certain legendary lovers such as Romeo and Juliet and Tristan and Isolde, and on more than one occasion he deserted his ship in order to be with his young love. He subsequently married Mary and their life together was one of devotion and mutual adoration, so much so that when she died he suffered a complete nervous collapse, failing to reconcile her death with his belief in a merciful God. He finally came to terms with it by interpreting his loss as a punishment visited on him for having loved a temporal being as much as his eternal master.

For John Newton saw the hand of God in everything. Even when a dissolute young sailor he was always mindful of omens, and inter-

11

preted many dangerous or discomforting moments as divine warnings. The second event that changed his life he interpreted as the final caveat. On a return journey from Africa where he had almost died of a fever, Newton plunged himself into one of his violent bouts of drinking and profanity. The ship he was on was subsequently beset by violent storms, and many of the sailors, convinced that the man they had rescued was bringing God's vengeance on their heads, demanded that he should be thrown overboard. Then on 9 March 1748, a day Newton never forgot till the day he died, the storms became so violent and the ship so near to sinking that Newton became finally convinced that God wished either to kill or cure him. He chose salvation, and from that day he became a deeply religious man.

But this was not the end of the paradoxical span of John Newton's life, for he now entered perhaps the most ambiguous chapter of his existence. Determined to marry Mary but utterly unable to afford it, he entered the slave trade as a seaman, knowing full well that it was the best and only way open to him to amass the necessary finance quickly. In that same year, 1748, he made his first slaving trip as a mate on a Guineaman, and on his return was sufficiently solvent to marry straightaway. Very soon he was made a captain and given the charge of a three-masted snow, the *Duke of Argyll*, owned by Mr Manesty of Liverpool.

In 1750 Newton's ship set sail from Liverpool, the richest and most prosperous of the slaving ports, for the coast of Africa on the first leg of the notorious three-legged run. She was crewed by the usual cross-section of men who were to be found serving on Guineamen, innocent young boys, their heads full of romantic notions of the African adventure, hardened sea-dogs on the run from gaol or working off pressing debts, deserters, criminals, and others tricked, drugged or kidnapped by the 'crimps' – men who specialised in getting sailors blind drunk and selling them while still unconscious to sea-going slave captains. The crew's lot was often even worse than that of the slaves their ship carried. Slaves fetched money once the ship reached the West Indies, but sailors were dispensable. Many a sailor, if he survived the rigours of the run, found himself abandoned in the West Indies by his homeward-bound captain. And of those that made it back to Liverpool, many were permanently crippled, blind, or doomed to die in the infirmaries.

Newton, however, was an honourable captain, and would attend to the needs of his men to the best of his ability. But as he set sail that year for the Coast, his holds full of cheap cloth, iron and copper bars, brandy, muskets, kettles, mirrors and glass beads, he knew full well that once more he would have to face the usual staggering loss of serving men. Not only would he have to endure the dangers from marauding privateers, but also suffer exposure to the African fevers to which white men were highly susceptible, and which would undoubtedly further decimate his crew.

While the *Duke of Argyll* was at sea, preparations were being made by dealers on the African coast. Slaving was a highly competitive affair, and by the middle of the eighteenth century, a well-organised one. Although British ships had the lion's share of the trade, the French, Dutch and Spaniards were also competing for slaves. Newton was sailing with enough cargo to purchase two hundred slaves and a ballast of ivory and camwood, but with the larger number of slavers plying the Coast for trade, slaves were very often in short supply, and this trip was to prove no exception.

Newton's principal contact on the Coast was a mulatto named Henry Tucker, half African, half Portuguese. He was a flamboyant character who had visited Europe, had several wives, and dined in his own native compound off European silver. Newton, in his journal, speaks highly of the trader's hospitality and of his honesty. Men like Tucker owed allegiance to neither African nor European and as middlemen they were valuable to both sides. But so far on this trip, by the time he entered into negotiations with Tucker, Newton had only managed to buy about a dozen slaves, and despite the usual extra offer of 'dash' – bribes of brandy, muskets and cloth – enough slaves were not immediately forthcoming. Anxious, as most captains were, to be slaved before the rains began, Newton was forced to send a longboat crewed by his second in command, Bridson, and four sailors up river in search of trade, a dangerous and unorthodox move.

While Bridson was away the *Duke of Argyll* prepared to receive her cargo. Once on board the slaves were stowed in a hold, measuring approximately fifteen foot by forty foot by five foot high, which was divided into two chambers for men and women by a rough bulkhead, and the chambers were again subdivided horizontally by slatted shelves so that there were two levels upon which the slaves were packed. And packed, although an emotive word, is exactly how the Africans were stowed away in these horrifically cramped quarters. Shackled to each other by heavy chains around their ankles they were forced to lie, not even sit, side by side during the long and terrible journey known as The Middle Passage, a trip whose average duration was about sixty days.

By the time the holds were full, the slaves would be wedged so tightly together that, unable to turn or sit, they could not even reach the inadequate latrine buckets in the far corners of the holds with the consequence that the wretched captives were forced to ease themselves where they lay. It was little wonder that it was said you could smell a slaver twenty miles downwind.

Many died before the ship ever left the coast, and Newton dutifully recorded every loss, 'this day buried a fine woman slave, no. 11 . . . she was taken with a lethargic disorder which they seldom recover from. Scraped the rooms, then smoked the ship with tar, tobacco and brimstone for two hours, afterwards washed with vinegar . . .'.

The effect on the Africans, many of them seeing the sea, ships and white men for the first time, must have been staggeringly traumatic. Many of them were convinced that they were to spend the rest of their days in these small wooden floating houses, or that the white men were going to eat them and drink their blood. So it is not at all surprising that so many died from sheer apathy and terror.

Captains slaving their ships did not only have to rely on dealers such as Tucker for supplies, nor indeed on the hazardous journeys upriver. Local kings were in the business, and the slave castles like Elmina and Anamaboe were already established, staffed by Europeans. By now it was common practice for African kings to raid unsuspecting adjacent villages in order to capture men and women whom they could then sell as slaves to the dealers. Some African tribes punished certain social offences, particularly adultery, with sentences of slavery. Also some would have been slaves already, for the African communities practised domestic slavery. Besides, individual Africans, tempted by the potential profit, were willing to sell their brothers into bondage for the price of a musket, a bottle of brandy or a leaking kettle. While the *Argyll* was laying at anchor waiting the first mate's return, one such native came on board with a young boy and girl for sale. The surgeon, Arthur, struck a bargain with him, valuing the children at two muskets, four kettles and a bolt of cloth. Arthur then signalled to the sailors to lay hands on the trader himself, but Newton, witnessing the commotion, ordered his immediate release, not from philanthropic zeal, but because he knew full well that such a greedy and foolish action could easily destroy his reputation as an honest captain. Besides, he wrote, '. . . it is politic to encourage Africans to enter the trade'.

Soon, Tucker sent word that a fresh coffle of slaves had arrived from the interior. Newton and Arthur were rowed across the bar to inspect the new arrivals. Newton observed the strict instructions he had received from his merchant, Manesty, to be choice in the buying of his slaves. So in the company of the haggling Tucker he selected those he

14

By 1721 — the date of the engraving below — 'castles'
were established up and down the West African coast

Cape Coast Castle (opposite top) and Elmina (below) illustrate
how these once small trading posts grew into multi-purpose
fortifications which housed governors, soldiers — and slaves
awaiting transportation to the Caribbean

thought would survive the journey and fetch a good price in the West Indies. He rejected the weak, the old, the ruptured, the sick, idiots and long-breasted women, paying only for those who, to his experienced eye, seemed strong and in good health, or those known to be artisans and craftsmen. Often those left behind at the trading posts were decapitated and their bodies thrown into the rivers if it seemed they were of no further use or interest to the buyers. They were seldom, if ever, allowed to go free. The ones that Newton had purchased were then branded with a hot iron, denoting they were now the property of Manesty & Co., and taken aboard.

By now Bridson had returned from up river, dying of yellow fever, with a feeble cargo of two captured women and one boy slave. He did not last long, 'Friday, 25 January . . . this day committed Mr Bridson's body to the sea . . . I shall regret his loss. His death will considerably retard my business . . . got up the spare sails out of the hold . . . the rats have done them a good deal of damage . . . we cannot get a cat upon any terms. Those we brought from England have been dead some time . . .'.

After three months of trading, the *Duke of Argyll* was almost fully loaded. Newton sold the longboat to Tucker for six more slaves, and exchanged two boys for a man and a woman slave to a Captain Williams who preferred to carry only children (common practice among certain captains who feared uprisings from maturer cargoes), he weighed anchor and set sail for the West Indies.

Newton always chose to leave the Coast at night, which although technically more dangerous, prevented a violent commotion among the two hundred slaves shackled below, because he had found a daylight departure panicked them fiercely. Those of the crew who had survived so far set about their work with great relief, for five of their number had already been lost, and seventeen of the slaves. Newton reminded his surgeon Arthur that there was a bounty for each slave delivered to Jamaica in good condition, but the young surgeon was already drinking heavily, having surrendered in his heart to the utter impossibility of ministering to any ailing or injured being lying in the

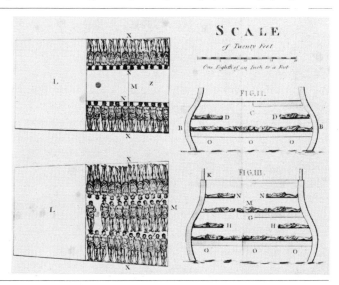

A slave 'coffle' in transit to the coast (opposite)

A cross section of the hold of a slave ship

darkness below. The most he could do was exercise the weak and the sick on deck, but when the 'flux', a most violent form of dysentery, established itself as it usually did among the slaves, there was nothing he was able to do for them. The heat, the stench, and the constant moaning in the holds were hard enough to stomach, but any attempt to walk amongst them and supervise their condition was rendered impossible by the cramped conditions and the perilously slimy state of the floors.

Arthur was not alone in his predilection for the state of insensibility induced by drink. The journey could be both monotonous and intolerable, and any captain found it difficult to keep his crew sober, if they had access to alcohol. A drunken crew could be dangerous both to the slaves and to the master of the ship. Newton often had to flog sailors he found attempting to violate the women slaves. Other captains had been murdered or incarcerated by mutinous crews, men made bloodily rebellious by the starvation diet they were forced to endure, or by the constant lack of drinking water. But the greatest danger to a safe journey lay in the holds below, because the sailors, weakened by the conditions of the journey, were outnumbered by their captives. Even Newton, the benevolent master, was aware of the constant danger of insurrection, and on this particular journey was faced with a revolt.

During a service conducted on deck for the crew, a small boy who was being exercised with a small group of fellow slaves, managed to smuggle a marlin spike to a companion below, who used it to break his shackles and those of his immediate neighbours. When this party in turn was brought up for exercise they attacked the unsuspecting crew, and if swift action had not been taken to prevent other slaves from getting up on deck, Newton might have found a very serious fight on his hands. As it was the slaves were easily overpowered. The ring-leader, to whom the boy had passed the spike, jumped overboard and drowned himself rather than face further captivity. The others were severely punished. Newton wrote, 'I did not think myself at liberty to dismiss the affair in silence . . . lest encouragement should be thereby given to such attempts . . . so I put the boy in irons, and slightly in the thumbscrews . . . to urge him to a full confession . . . I resolve to entertain no personal hatred or ill-will . . . I can sincerely say . . . that I have endeavoured to do my duty by them without oppression . . . ill language or any kind of abuse . . . remembering that I also have a Master in Heaven . . . and there is no respecter of persons with him . . .'

Ironically enough, a defeated mutiny among the slaves was ultimately to their advantage, because any successful uprising was tantamount to signing their own mass death warrant. For none of the captured Africans had the remotest idea of how to sail a ship, and whenever they gained control of a vessel, it just drifted helplessly about the ocean until the slaves all died of starvation and thirst. Perhaps the majority would have preferred this as an end to their miserable existence, and certainly many attempts at individual suicide were made on the journeys.

Some, like the Coramantee who led the revolt on Newton's ship, would drown themselves at sea, and were often observed to raise their hands above their heads as they went under as if in exultation. Reports of breath holding were made, but perhaps the most common attempt at suicide was made by refusing food. This was dealt with easily, though severely. The culprit was forced to his knees and a red hot coal was applied to his mouth to make him scream. Then a device known as the Speculum Oris was inserted in his mouth which forcibly

Descending from M'banis to the plain.

Although these two illustrations of slaves being taken to the coast
are from a later date, the modes of transportation did not change

'Scene on the coast of Africa' by A. F. Biard

BRANDING A NEGRESS.

The frontispiece to Theodore Canot's memoirs, *Twenty Years A Slaver*, 1854, and silver branding irons with slave owners' initials

held it open while food was emptied into the victim's gullet. The whip was often applied simultaneously to underline the seriousness of the offence. Any misdemeanour was punished by flogging or torture, and the sick and ailing, if nothing further could be done to redeem them, were 'requested' to jump overboard.

It has been argued that these atrocities visited by white man on black during the slave runs have been exaggerated both at the time by the abolitionists, and more recently by historians. It has been rightly stated that conditions on all the slavers were not as horrific as this, and that many captains and sailors showed kindness to their captives. Indeed some captains have passed into folklore as benefactors of the captured Africans. Captain Crow by his own account, enjoyed the trust and admiration of his live cargo, so much so that crowds of negroes were reported to have rushed aboard his ship to greet their old friend every time he docked in Jamaica. But Captain Crow was never the most reliable of witnesses, and the facts speak more than amply for themselves.

The tolerable loss to the slavers a journey was $12\frac{1}{2}\%$. Calamitous losses, such as 375 slaves surviving out of a total of 700 (the *Hannibal*), 90 out of 219 (the Dutch *St Jan*), or 214 out of 339 (the *Greyhound*), were not uncommon. For the Middle Passage alone, an average of 13% of slaves were lost. Add to this the losses before ships left the coast ($4\frac{1}{2}\%$) and losses at the other end during the 'seasoning period', when slaves were broken in (33%), and losses total just over 50%. This would mean, if these figures are accurate, that each single slave working in the New World was imported at the cost of the life of another.

Naturally captains were aware of the value of their cargo, and steps were taken on the journey to keep alive as many slaves as possible. The slaves were exercised to the whip and even to music, and kept on a bulk diet of maize porridge, rice, millet and horse beans, the last of which, incidentally, the negroes abhorred. More often than not the diet was reduced to fatty water with a few horse beans floating in it. No captain would willingly be rid of his cargo while at sea unless the safety of his ship was endangered. Consequently, the crew were more dispensable, and as the ship drew nearer its destination, conditions were made even more intolerable for the crew so that they could be forced to desert in the West Indies, where they would become the riff-raff of the waterfront. This also saved the employers having to pay their wages, as a deserter forfeited the right of being paid.

But if the crew suffered a higher proportional mortality rate, their living conditions on the journey were in no way as bad as the slaves.

And it also must be remembered that the majority of the sailors worked on the Guineamen voluntarily. The men, women and children taken to the New World were stolen from their homes and villages to supply cheap labour for white economy. None of them had volunteered to spend weeks lying in their own ordure while their companions died of dysentery, smallpox, or opthalmia. None of the many pregnant black women kidnapped from their villages would willingly have offered to spend the terminal period of their gestation and the hours of their labour shackled to dead men whom the sailors on board had been too neglectful to remove. No young girl or boy from the civilised villages of Ibo, who practised a strict sexual code, wished to prostitute their formative years satisfying the carnal needs of the white men at sea or at home in the plantations. These people were involuntary immigrants, and this was one of the aspects of the trade that so persistently bothered Captain Newton and subsequently the men and women concerned with abolition and emancipation. Newton later wrote, 'during the time I was engaged in the slave trade I never had the least scruple as to its lawfulness . . . I often petitioned in my prayers that the Lord in his own time would be pleased to fix me in a more humane calling.' His supplication was to be granted, and he was to become one of the significant figures in the fight against slavery.

Once Newton had quelled the uprising on his ship, the rest of his journey passed uneventfully. Losses on the voyage were average, twenty-eight blacks and seven of his crew, including the surgeon, Arthur, who died on the journey home. During the latter half of the dreaded Middle Passage, Newton's journal makes melancholy reading: 'Friday, 7 June, departed this life, Gideon Masham . . . of a fever . . . Wednesday, 12 June, buried a man slave, no. 84, of a flux . . . Thursday, 13 June, buried a woman slave, no. 47 . . . know not what to say she died of for she has not been properly alive since she first came on board . . . Thursday, 20 June, buried two slaves, a man, no. 140, of a flux, and a boy, no. 170, of the gravel and stoppage of urine . . . Saturday, 22 June . . . have seen two or three tropic birds and a few flying fish . . . Monday, 24 June . . . buried a boy slave, no. 158, of a flux . . . Friday, 28 June . . . buried a girl slave, no. 172, of a flux . . .' The second slave purchased was almost the last to die, 'Saturday, 29 June, buried a man slave, no. 2, of a flux he has sustained about three months . . . Monday, 1 July, buried a man slave, no. 36, of a flux . . . I begin to think long for the land . . .' So it was with great relief and much thanksgiving that he espied the West Indian coastline, and fired a salvo to announce his arrival.

The arrival of a slaver in the West Indies was an occasion for much activity, both professional and social. The plantations in the Caribbean had grown in an astonishingly short time from relatively small holdings to estates averaging 1000 acres and valued in millions. By the middle of the eighteenth century the value of sugar as a raw material can only be compared to that of oil in contemporary markets, and being free from any crippling excise duty, fortunes could be made from its mass production. And it was this very need for the mass production of sugar cane that transformed the face of the West Indian plantations. Mass production needed cheap labour and the windward coast of Africa supplied the perfect work-force. Even before 1540, 1000 slaves were being imported annually into their Caribbean colonies by the Spaniards, and in 1690 there were 40,000 slaves in Jamaica alone. One hundred years later, at the height of the trade, 800,000 more had been imported. It is impossible to exaggerate the importance that the production of sugar had on the British economy, and at its zenith the West Indian islands in British possession dominated the social, political and economic life of England. In 1778 the plantations were worth a conservative £70 million, and the affluence of the sugar magnates dazzled London society, prompting the Abbé Raynal to remark that the West Indies 'may be considered the principal cause of the rapid motion which now stimulates the universe.'

Newton landed at St John's in Antigua, and when he stepped ashore to open negotiations, he had no qualms about the success of the impending sale. When times were bad slave captains sometimes had to peddle their wares around the islands, often being forced to sell at ridiculously low prices, or off-load their cargo to a 'soul driver', who in turn would trail his piteous caravan around the plantations in the hope of effecting piecemeal transactions. But when business was good, as it was this year, high prices could be expected for the slaves either at an auction, or at a 'scramble'.

John Newton had made sure before leaving his ship for land, that the usual precautions were being taken in order to make his surviving cargo as presentable as possible. This was difficult after a particularly bad voyage when it was sometimes impossible to differentiate between the living and the dead in the holds. But whenever possible, the two or three days prior to the auction were used to patch up the damage wrought on the slaves by the rigours of the Middle Passage. Their shackles were hacked off and any ulcers that may have formed beneath them were rubbed over with iron rust, their bodies were oiled and fattened up with food brought from ashore, and any incontinent slave had to suffer the indignity of having his rectum stuffed with cork or tow. None of these measures were ever wholly successful, for any

27

Insurrections, which were commonplace, were infrequently successful. Even if the slaves gained control of the ship they had no knowledge of sailing and consequently the ship would drift out of control and the rebels would die protracted and agonising deaths from starvation, thirst, and disease

REPRESENTATION of an INSURRECTION on board
A SLAVE-SHIP.

Shewing how the crew fire upon the unhappy Slaves from behind the BARRICADO, erected on board all Slave ships, as a security whenever such commotions may happen.

See the privy council's report part I. Art: SLAVES.
Minutes of evidence before the House of Commons.
Wadstrom's Essay on Colonization §. 471.

Watercolour of the hold of a captured slaver, done on the spot
by a young English naval officer

In the Middle Passage one of the problems facing captains was to allow the slaves
any reprieve from the foul conditions of their berths. One common way of 'exercising'
the human cargoes was to force the captives to dance — to the
accompaniment of the whip (opposite)

survivor always bore the marks of his horrific journey, but the buyers were now used to spotting the ones who would fatten up well and make strong servants.

By now, the planters were also selective about which of the Africans they paid good money for, paying top fees for Wydah natives, and the Mandingoes. The Ibos fetched less because of their supposed suicidal tendencies, and the Congolese and Angolans were thought to be stupid. There is much mention in the literature of slavery of the Coromantees. They were supposed to be strong and active, but dangerous men, being antipathetic to discipline, and quick to rouse. The Spaniards and French were supposed to be terrified of them and would not willingly purchase them. But in fact there is not and never was a tribe called Coromantee. There is a village called Kromantyn (Coromentee) near a ruined castle on the coast of Ghana. Coromantee was not a nation but a brand-name. In the dungeons of such castles, Africa died and America began.

Newton was greeted on shore by the representative of Newton's employer in Liverpool, who reassured the captain that the market was good and the price healthy, about £55 a head. The policy adopted by the planters of working the slaves very hard for a few years and then replacing them had made the turnover higher, and the need for slaves therefore even greater. Unfortunately for Newton, due to the length of the journey and the persistence of the 'flux' his cargo were not in the best state to be auctioned immediately, so the agent recommended sale by 'scramble'.

At a straightforward auction the slaves would be herded into a room or hall and the buyers would inspect them at their leisure and bid for them in an orthodox manner, a process that must have been sufficient both to baffle and frighten the slaves. But at a scramble they must have thought all their worst fears about savage man-eating white men were about to be realised. For the slaves were herded into a compound, and then at a given signal the doors would be opened and the buyers, overseers and headmen would rush in and grab as many of the slaves as they could, by means of surrounding them with ropes, or chains, or even plaits made of their handkerchieves. They would then pay for as many head as they had captured and take them away to the plantation. No attempt was ever made to keep families, tribes or even shipmates together. In fact this was actively discouraged and was an important part of the planter's 'seasoning' policy.

Once the slaves were successfully sold, Newton's final responsibility lay in stocking his ship with her third and most valuable cargo, the produces of slave labour, namely sugar, tobacco, mahogany, rum and spices, which gave the merchant back home in England his third profit from the same voyage. The three-legged run, politely known as the triangular trade, was one of the most ingenious devices for making money in commerce ever invented. The first and cheapest cargo paid for the slaves in Africa, and the slaves paid for the valuable goods returned to England, so that it was profit all the way. On this journey, Manesty and Co., Newton's merchant employers, would clear £15,000 which was about the average expectation at that time, and of which Newton could expect five per cent. For the master of the ships, the last leg of the voyage was the least hazardous, so he could afford some social relaxation while his ship was being loaded and prepared.

The planters at this time were rich and fairly idle. If that year's crop was good, they could afford to do little, since their estates were run by a well-ordered system of ganging organised by their overseers and headmen. The planters lived in large houses, built at a good distance from the plantation villages and downwind so that they need not be troubled by the odours of their employees. They were well spread out through the islands, so when a neighbouring planter and his family came to visit they stayed for several days, and all parties would gorge and drink themselves insensible. There was little else for the planters to do. They were not concerned with the welfare of their slaves, nor were they interested in improving the general amenities of the islands upon which they had settled. Few built chapels or schools, and no attempt was made to educate the slaves lest they should gain any knowledge which might lead them to be critical of their wretched lot. And as the trade prospered, the plantations were inclined to be owned by absentee landlords, and run by rough, ignorant managers whose only interest was to make a swift profit and then return to the comforts of England. The growth of sugar was by nature a hazardous occupation, and should the crop fail, which it frequently did, that year could be a brutally hard one for all concerned.

Newton was witness on several occasions to the appalling cruelty of the planters and the overall barbarity of the plantation system. Every time he was entertained by these men, as indeed he was on this voyage, and listened to their harangues against the negroes whose involuntary labour was making them rich, he increasingly felt that not only would any further personal participation in such a trade be wrong, but that the very system itself could no longer be supported by anyone who professed to be a practising Christian. But true to his character, it was not until he received what he believed to be the final Divine signal that he at last divorced himself from the business of slaving.

In England, after his third voyage as a captain, he was struck down

31

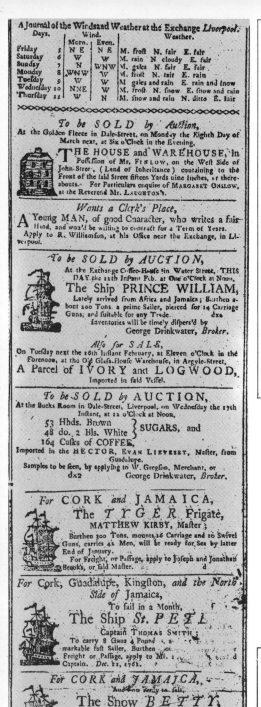

A Journal of the Winds and Weather at the Exchange *Liverpool.*

Days.	Morn. Wind	Even. Wind	Weather.
Friday 5	N E	N E	M. frost N. fair E. fair
Saturday 6	W	W	M. rain N. cloudy E. fair
Sunday 7	N	WNW	M. gales N. fair E. fair
Monday 8	WNW	W	M. frost N. fair E. rain
Tuesday 9	W	W	M. gales and rain E. rain and snow
Wednesday 10	NNE	W	M. frost N. snow E. snow and rain
Thursday 11	W	W	M. snow and rain N. ditto E. fair

To be SOLD by Auction,

At the Golden Fleece in Dale-Street, on Monday the Eighth Day of March next, at Six o'Clock in the Evening,

THE HOUSE and WAREHOUSE, in Possession of Mr. Finlow, on the West Side of John-Street, (Land of Inheritance) containing to the Front of the said Street fifteen Yards nine Inches, or thereabouts. For Particulars enquire of Margaret Onslow, at the Reverend Mr. Laughton's.

Wants a Clerk's Place,

A Young MAN, of good Character, who writes a fair Hand, and would be willing to contract for a Term of Years. Apply to R. Williamson, at his Office near the Exchange, in Liverpool.

To be SOLD by AUCTION,

At the Exchange Coffee-House in Water Street, THIS DAY the 12th Instant Feb. at One o'Clock at Noon,

The Ship PRINCE WILLIAM,

Lately arrived from Africa and Jamaica, a prime Sailer, about 200 Tons, pierced for 14 Carriage Guns; and suitable for any Trade.

Inventories will be timely dispers'd by
George Drinkwater, Broker.

Also for SALE,

On Tuesday next the 16th Instant February, at Eleven o'Clock in the Forenoon, at the Old Glass-House Warehouse, in Argyle-Street,

A Parcel of IVORY and LOGWOOD, Imported in said Vessel.

To be SOLD by AUCTION,

At the Bucks Room in Dale-Street, Liverpool, on Wednesday the 17th Instant, at 12 o'Clock at Noon,

53 Hhds. Brown
48 do. 2 Bls. White } SUGARS, and
164 Casks of COFFEE,

Imported in the HECTOR, Evan Lievesey, Master, from Guadalupe.

Samples to be seen, by applying to W. Gregson, Merchant, or
George Drinkwater, Broker.

For CORK and JAMAICA,

The TYGER Frigate,
MATTHEW KIRBY, Master;

Burthen 300 Tons, mounts 16 Carriage and 10 Swivel Guns, carries 42 Men, will be ready for Sea by latter End of January.

For Freight, or Passage, apply to Joseph and Jonathan Brooks, or said Master.

For Cork, Guadalupe, Kingston, and the North Side of Jamaica,

To sail in a Month,
The Ship St. PETER,

Captain THOMAS SMITH;

To carry 8 Guns 4 Pound, a remarkable fast Sailer, Burthen. For Freight, or Passage, apply to Mr. or Captain. Dec. 11, 1761.

For CORK and JAMAICA,

And now ready to sail,
The Snow BETTY,

WILLIAM OWEN, Master;

Carries a Letter of Marque, 8 Carriage Guns, 8 of them Six Pounders in Close Quarters. For Freight or Passage, apply to Mr. Richard Savage, Merchant.

Letters of Marque for Private Ships of War,

AND

PROTECTIONS from the Press,

FOR

Ships Companies, Apprentices, Sailors upwards of Fifty-five Years of Age, Foreigners, and Landmen, that intend going to Sea, may be had with the greatest Expedition, by applying to
THOMAS STATHAM, Postmaster at Liverpool.

Sales of 268 Negro Slaves imported in the Ship A... Captain Thomas Trader from Malemba on the Acct & Risque of Mess.rs John Cole and Co Owners of the said Ship, Merch... in Liverpool

To whom sold	Men	Women	Boys	Girls	Total	Price £
By James Fisher		1		1		35
John Miller	1				1	35
Augustus Valette	1				1	40
George Richards	1				1	35
Ditto	1				1	35
Paplay & Wade	103	26	67	34	230 @	7820
Chambers & Mead	5		2	1	8 @	296
Sloop Two Brothers			6		6 @	204
Mons.r Fontanelle				2	2 @ 36£	72
John Darcy		2			2 @ 30£	60
Ditto	4	3	2	3	12 @ 35£	420
Alexan Forceston	1			1	2 Sickly	30
Sold at Vendue		1			1 Capt to acct for	
	112	30	85	41	268	9082

Charges Viz.

		£ S D
To cash paid Import Duty, 268 Slaves @ 10.. Bond		134 5 0
To ditto paid the Doctor his head money on ditto @ 12		13 8
To ditto paid Captain Trader his Coast Commiss		349 6 2
@ 4£ @ 104 on 9082£ Gross Sales		
To my Commission @ 5£ p Cent on the Gross Sales		454 2
		951 1

To Mess.rs John Cole & Co: Owners of the African in Acct Curr.t for nt ... 8130 16

Errors Excepted
Kingston Jamaica 19 Sept 1764
p Wm Boyd

Documents of the trade:
the advertisements on the left are from
Williamson's Liverpool Advertiser, 1761

Negroes for Sale.

A Cargo of very fine stout Men and Women, in good order and fit for immediate service, just imported from the Windward Coast of A... ca, in the Ship Two Brothers. Conditions are one half Cash or Produce, the other half payable the first of January next, giving Bond and Security if required.

The Sale to be opened at 10 o'Clock each Day in Mr. Bourdeaux's Yard, at No. 48, on the Bay.
May 19, 1784. JOHN MITCHELL

by an apoplectic fit. When he recovered, he vowed to do God's will only, and subsequently joined the Ministry. He was ordained in 1764, and spent his first sixteen years at the parish of Olney where, with the poet Cowper, he wrote and published the Olney hymns. Then a wealthy friend, Henry Thornton, himself an abolitionist, gave him the living of St Mary Woolnoth in the City of London. Newton became famous for his impassioned sermons, and his church was a meeting place for abolitionists. Wilberforce himself came to him for spiritual counsel. Newton campaigned against the trade until he died in the year of its abolition, 1807.

One of the saddest and often unrealised aspects of the slave trade was the
consequent annihilation of African culture. Surviving works of art give some idea
of the quality of what was destroyed

This Benin bronze plaque (facing) and Yoruba carving of a horseman
are from Nigeria

2. One Man's Property

'Thy bond men and bond maids shall be of the
heathen that are around you, of them shall ye
buy bond men and bond maids.'

(Leviticus.)

In order to enslave the negro it was necessary to despise him. Many of
our contemporary racial fears and prejudices are directly inherited
from the so-called Age of Enlightenment when black people were
considered not as human beings but as goods and chattels, and this
attitude was given respectability by both law and religion.

In 1765 there was a notorious case in London which radically
altered the legal situation. But the very foundation of the establishment, the Church, not only refused to condemn slavery but actively
encouraged its practise and its survival. The text from Leviticus,
quoted above, was a great favourite in the pulpits of Bristol and Liverpool, and in the colonies the bishops and their clergy would buy and
employ black labour and, much worse, would refuse baptism to any
negro slave who might request it, because 'the established church did
not recognise them as baptisable human beings'. It was left to the
dissenting churches, the Quakers, Baptists, and the much derided
Methodists to oppose slavery while the Church of England was still
busy extolling its virtues. It is against this religious background that
we find the first clue to the theory of the 'respectability' of slavery. For
it was widely held that the primitives discovered in the dark wilds of
the mysterious continent were the 'Children of Ham'. They appeared
to the European eye to be little above animals, except of course for
their unusual propensity for physical work. Their very design seemed
to fit the purpose of enslavement and thus the curse of Ham was at
last 'satisfactorily' translated. And since the Church not only failed to
condemn the commerce but was actively justifying it, who then would
oppose it?

As traders and explorers travelled deeper into Africa, tales of
atrocities among the natives began to filter back. Stories of human
sacrifices, genocide, and mass torture gave further proof to the growing notion that the black man was a bloodthirsty savage, and justification to the belief that slavery was his natural state. Little attention was

37

modern photograph
the Omanhene of Akrokerri
lebrating the Yam Festival

paid to any reports of civilised communities like Benin, Kano or Kumasi, and no attempt was made to understand the African culture the white men were so blindly destroying. The slave trade was depriving Africa of her best workers, and substituting for her native arts and crafts the cheap manufactured goods of Europe. It is true that some African tribes offered human sacrifices, but was this a more appalling example of barbarity than flogging a slave to death or tossing live cargoes to the sharks? At least the African performed his sacrifices out of religious zeal. The white man sacrificed his cargo for the insurance money.

So the myth of the ignorant savage grew, and the belief in his inferiority hardened. By the time they reached the plantations the slaves were viewed purely as instruments of work, and as animals that had to be broken. In the colonies there was a general antipathy towards the blacks, and they were accused of being stupid, ugly, mistrustful, dishonourable, thievish, crafty and murderous. Edward Long, an extremist admittedly, announced in his *History of Jamaica* that the blacks had a 'bestial and fetid smell', and that 'ludicrous as the opinion may seem I do not think an orangoutang would be any dishonour to

It was a widely held belief in the eighteenth century that the 'primitives' of Africa were the children of Ham. Customs and tribal rites such as the Yam Festival which then

an Hottentot female'. They were condemned for having the morals of pigs, but since the slave men outnumbered the women by six to one, it is understandable that there was a high incidence of homosexuality among them. And it was also then that the fallacies – still believed by many today – that black men were better equipped sexually and that their women gave birth with little trouble and no pain, enjoyed great popularity. In short, it was often claimed that transportation to the beautiful islands of the West Indies, and the opportunity to serve white masters was the best thing that could be done for the unfortunate African.

Not long after John Newton's fit and 'conversion', an irascible lawyer named David Lisle set sail from Barbados with his family and entourage, which included a black manservant named Jonathan Strong. Strong was to feature centrally in a case which was to challenge the British legal attitude to domestic slavery. Lisle may have been leaving life on the plantations with some regret, but his wife would undoubtedly have been glad to see the back of the islands and return to the glamorous English social scene. In the West Indies at that time social life was practically non-existent, and there was little

included human sacrifice served to give credence to that belief. This illustration of European officers watching the festival is from Bowdich's *Mission to Ashantee*, 1819

for the women to do except prepare vast orgies of eating. Most of the planters or plantation managers were brutish and unintelligent, and most of the women were miserable so far from home. Perhaps because of the infinite boredom of their existence many of the womenfolk were more sadistic towards the slaves than the men, on occasions ordering their female servants to be flogged merely to 'brisk' them up a bit.

The male planters often indulged themselves wantonly with the desirable negresses, some of them even forcing their slave girls into prostitution so that they could confiscate their earnings for a little extra pocket money. Another favourite pastime enjoyed by the whites was a ritual called 'washing a blackamoor white', that is 'intriguing with the mother, the daughter, granddaughter etc. till the black colour disappear'.

David Lisle would have been the exception if he had not pleasured himself with his young female slaves, though if any black male slave had shown the slightest inclination to favour his wife or any other white woman Lisle would have flogged him insensible. Whatever the cause, it is a matter of record that Strong had suffered many a brutal flogging from his sadistic master.

Strong would have been relieved to be spared further miseries on the islands, for although there were some plantations where more benevolent masters attended to the needs of their slaves with a degree of humanity and concern, these were exceptions. The general rule was that from the moment the slaves arrived in the West Indies their spirits must be broken. This was achieved first by the separation of tribes, kinsmen, friends and families, the result of which was that the transported Africans lost their own languages and thus much of their own culture, and were forced to adopt the language of their masters in order to communicate even with each other. The next step in the seasoning was their introduction to the exhausting system of working the plantations and the sugar mills. They were flogged, driven and brainwashed until their life in Africa must have seemed as distant from them as any thoughts of future happiness. Many Africans believed that they had 'died' anyway when they left Africa on the slave ships, so consequently many more of them expired from the 'lethargic disorders' when faced with the living death of field and boiling house. It has been estimated that thirty per cent of the new slaves died during the first three years, for many of the Africans, weakened by their journey and dispirited by their prospects, had neither the will nor the strength to fulfil the required work rate and survive the regular floggings.

The whip was used for punishment and as a stimulant to labour, so floggings were plentiful. To the planter there was no other satisfactory

Once on the plantations the whip was the badge of slavery – and the most common
form of punishment

form of major punishment. He could slit a slave's tongue, or his nose,
castrate him or put him in the collar – a wicked device widely used
because the enormous spikes which protruded from the padlocked
necklace not only prevented the miscreant from sleeping but also from
running away because the spikes would get fouled in the bush – but he
could not fine him because the slave was paid no wages. So the slave
was flogged, often so mercilessly that a finger could be laid in the
wheals on his back. Even the flogging of a pregnant woman presented
no difficulty. A hole was dug to accommodate the belly, and she was
then laid prone to be beaten. Planters who were loath to chastise
their slaves personally could hire a professional flogger or 'jumper' to
carry out the punishments. The law stipulated a maximum of thirty-
nine strokes, but it did not stipulate the length of time between successive punishments, and anyway nobody paid much attention to the
legalities of flogging. The law of the islands disallowed any black person to give evidence in court if they were still enslaved, so if a negro
died from his punishment it was impossible to collect evidence against
his murderer. Mutiny, the most serious offence, was punishable by
death, and the modes of execution were chosen for their deterrent
value rather than for their expediency. Slow burning was common, as
was hanging the condemned slave up to 'dry' in an iron cage.

It was only to be expected, therefore, that many of the slaves became

Francis Barber (*c.* 1740–1801), Dr Johnson's manservant, who entered his service in 1752 and was his principal legatee

apathetic and did not live long. Their refusal to breed in captivity further irritated their employers, since many of them looked forward to being able to boast a self-regenerating cycle of slave labour. But the negresses were skilful in the use of herb pessaries and of the rhythm method. Infant mortality among the slave women was shockingly high, their children often being still born or fatally infected with neonatal tetanus, the 'jawfall'. Even as the slaves grew old there was little hope of a relaxation of the hard regime imposed upon them during their working lives. Few were pensioned off. Many were turned out off the plantations, or onto the streets to beg, put on reduced rations, or even, as was the habit of one notorious planter, framed for crimes they had not committed so that they could be executed and the legal compensation due to the master for the death of a slave by lawful destruction could be claimed. On Sundays, the slaves were required to cultivate their own food, and Christmas was the only holiday. Although many visitors to the colonies remarked on the cheerfulness of the slaves, and enjoyed their seemingly happy habit of breaking into song and dance, these reports would seem to be proof, not of good treatment, but of the resilience of the human spirit. It is interesting to note that in the generation after emancipation the birth rate among the black population of the West Indies sharply and dramatically increased.

So when Jonathan Strong reached England he would have been astounded by the comparatively soft existence of the black and white servants of the nobility. He would have learned of the existence of such beings as free black men, like Dr Johnson's manservant, Francis Barber. Dr Johnson himself, though a Tory, delighted in baiting the planters by publicly toasting 'the next insurrection in the West Indies,' and arguing that although the civilisations of the past had been built on slavery, it would be an even greater achievement to build one without it.

Mrs Lisle, fresh from the stultefying tedium of Barbados, would have been astounded by the glittering display of wealth achieved by her fellow 'West Indians'. An example of this was the enormous mansion at Fonthill, the country estate of William Beckford, Lord Mayor of London, who boasted an income of £150,000 a year from his Jamaican estates. Mrs Lisle would have been amazed by the public display of affection shown by the Duchess of Devonshire to her black lover, Soubise. For although it was fashionable to have powdered and bewigged black servants dressed in fine array as personal attendants and perhaps occasionally as paramours, it was only a voguish indulgence and notions of equality or liberty were not seriously entertained. Most businessmen, merchants and politicians were bitterly opposed to the importation of black slaves from the West Indies into England. Their arguments, eloquently expressed by Edward Long in *Candid Reflections*, echo the racist sentiments of today: 'The lower class of women in England are remarkably fond of the blacks, for reasons too brutal to mention; they would connect themselves with horses and asses if the laws permitted them. By these ladies they generally have a numerous brood. Thus, in the course of a few generations more, the English blood will become so contaminated with this mixture . . . till the whole nation resembles the Portuguese and Moriscos in complexion of skin and baseness of mind . . .' And again, '. . . the multiplication of Negro domestics tends in a very final degree to defeat the wise and good purposes of these laws, since it excludes an equal number of poor white natives from that bread to which they are entitled by a prior claim . . .'

But now, with the arrival of David Lisle and his servant Strong, the national feelings concerning the state of slavery in England were about to be tested. Already the intellectual climate was changing, and a more liberal attitude towards the black man was slowly coming into being, initiated by the voyages of such adventurers as Tasman, Anson and

Cook, romanticised by such best-selling fiction as Robinson Crusoe, and strengthened by the conception of the 'noble savage' as popularised by Rousseau. Humanism was finding its feet, and the intellectual vocabulary was alive with words such as 'unalienable rights', 'reform', 'democracy', and the slogan of the French Revolution, 'liberté, egalité, fraternité'. This awakening conscience was leading some people to examine the very ethics of slavery, particularly when it was brought to their attention that slave auctions were being held quite brazenly in England. Slaves often escaped from their masters to seek refuge and sometimes baptism in the British Islands. Chief Justice Holt had encouraged this by ruling that in law a negro slave upon entering England became free, and many argued that baptised negroes could not be forced by their masters to return to the plantations. But the West Indian interests had pressed for a legal judgement on this matter which would favour them, and they achieved it through the joint opinion of Yorke and Talbot in 1749 which ruled that any residency in England or baptism of slaves on these islands did not make them exempt from a compulsory return to the plantations if their masters demanded it.

Granville Sharp rescuing the slave Strong. This reconstruction was painted by James Hayllar in 1864, at the suggestion of Richard Cobden

So it was not until sixteen years later, when David Lisle flogged and pistol whipped his manservant Jonathan Strong on some trumped up pretext, and threw him out onto the London streets, that a real opportunity was found to obtain a legal reversal of this position.

Strong, although extremely badly injured about the head and chest, was fortunate, because although a complete stranger to the byways of London, he somehow found his way to the surgery of Dr William Sharp down in Mincing Lane, and his arrival outside the surgery in the East End was to prove a turning point in history. The Sharp family was already famous in London circles, William being surgeon to the King, and James one of the pioneers of the inland waterway system. They were a closely knit and devoted family, loved for their humanity and for their exceptional musical abilities. Granville Sharp, who when leaving the surgery that day after visiting his brother discovered the semi-conscious and battered negro on the doorstep, was the twelfth of fourteen brothers, and at this time a minor clerk in the obscure office of Ordnance in the Tower. But there was nothing minor about his ability, for as a teenager he had demonstrated his exceptional scholarship by mastering both Greek and Hebrew, and was now also considered to be an extremely talented flautist and oboist. But until he rescued Strong and with the aid of his brother William, secured a place for the injured man in St Bartholomew's hospital where the slave could receive the treatment, Granville Sharp's interest in slavery had been minimal. Now he was to turn all his energies and resources first to fighting the case of Jonathan Strong, and then the case for the total abolition of slavery. He was to become known as the father of the abolition movement, but it needed one more turn of the screw before he was fully impelled into action.

Strong recovered after three months in hospital and a month's convalescence with the Sharps, and the brothers found him a job as errand boy for a chemist in Fenchurch Street. And there the matter might have rested had not David Lisle, passing in his carriage some two years later, recognised Strong in the street. He followed and recaptured him, and then promptly sold the unfortunate Strong to a Jamaica planter, James Kerr. Kerr, wishing to keep his property safe, threw Strong into gaol at Poultry Counter Prison until his ship was due to sail, which was as it turned out both an illegal and unfortunate action. Strong, highly distressed, managed to get a message through to Granville Sharp, seeking his help, and Sharp (once he had remembered who the sender of the letter was) went to the Poultry Counter and heard from Strong verbatim what had occurred.

Sharp, in his *Memoirs*, described what followed: '. . . The boy was detained without charge or warrant. I insisted that the Lord Mayor summon those persons who had detained him, and in my presence! . . . on the appointed day, there was no one there but a notary with a bill of sale for the lad and a ship's captain to take him away. The Lord Mayor, having heard the claim, says, the lad has not stolen anything, is not guilty of any offence, and is at liberty to go. Whereupon . . . the captain seizes him by the arm, and claims him as the *property* of Mr

Granville
Sharp, in
1794, by
G. Dance

Kerr . . . Mr Beech, the coroner, comes behind me, and whispers in my ear "charge him" . . . at which, I turned upon the captain . . ."Sir! I charge *you* for an assault!" On this, the captain quits his hold of Jonathan's arm, we all bow to the Lord Mayor, and come away, Jonathan following me, and no one daring to touch him.'

But David Lisle and James Kerr were bent on revenge against the meddlesome clerk who had interfered in their business so successfully. Having first challenged Granville Sharp to a duel, which was lightly but politely refused, Lisle then set about suing him for damages, and such seemed to be the strength of his legal argument that Sharp's lawyers advised their client to drop the case, and settle out of court. They reminded him of the opinion of Yorke and Talbot, and stressed that even Lord Mansfield, who was to become Sharp's greatest legal adversary, had confirmed this opinion several times in the King's

Lord Mansfield, in 1783, by J. S. Copley

Bench. The planters felt supremely confident that their ill-equipped opponent would settle out of court and leave the wretched Strong to his inevitable fate, but they had sadly misjudged their opponent. Granville Sharp, seeing the possible ramifications of the case, and unable to believe that English law could be so unjust in this matter, decided immediately to make a full and proper study of the law and to conduct his own defence. For two years he studied and prepared his

47

argument, and then finally published his memorandum, which re-quoted Justice Holt's judgement (that there could be no such things as slaves in England) and supported it fully with a watertight legal argument, which rested ultimately on Magna Carta. Mansfield advised Lisle to withdraw, because that way only one slave would be lost, while if the case went to full trial and judgement was found against Lisle and Kerr, it could upset a very sizeable applecart.

But that was exactly what Sharp was intent on doing, and he found little satisfaction in Lisle's withdrawal. He was determined to get an absolute ruling from Mansfield, so he did not let the case rest there. Mansfield, for his part, suspected that Sharp's memorandum was tell-ing an uncomfortable truth, that in fact there was no legal justification for slavery in this country. But he dreaded the consequences of so ruling for at this time there were as many as twenty thousand slaves in England, brought over to England by planters secure in the belief that their property was protected by law. A decision found for Sharp would free these people onto the streets without any maintenance, and also lose the influential planters property worth £700,000. So Mansfield dreaded the inevitable confrontation.

Sharp, of course, was eagerly anticipating it, and although techni-cally losing out to Mansfield in two or three preliminary skirmishes, in 1772 he was afforded his best opportunity to date, when the case of the slave James Somerset was brought to his attention. Somerset had been brought to England from Virginia by Charles Stewart, his master, and like so many before him he had attempted to run away rather than return to plantation life. But his attempt had been unsuccessful, Stewart had recaptured him and he had been sold for transportation back to the West Indies. Sharp served a writ of habeas corpus on the captain of the ship which was waiting to take Somerset across the Atlantic, and battle commenced. By now the West Indian interests were extremely worried as to the possible outcome of this war of legal attrition between the ordnance clerk and the Lord Chief Justice, so they plunged a lot of money into securing the very best legal aid for their side. But Sharp was extremely confident, because he sensed that his old adversary was by now becoming convinced that he was wrong and that Sharp was right. The public were enthralled as well, and the court was packed to hear the argument out. They had already been witness to the most recent case Sharp had fought, that of the slave Lewis, when he had narrowly failed to obtain the ruling he so desper-ately sought. Mansfield had avoided a decision in that case by securing from the jury a verdict that Lewis was not his master's property, and therefore he had refused to consider the wider issues

48

unless it could be proved otherwise. He had ended that case with a note of warning: 'I don't know what the consequences may be if the masters were to lose their property by accidentally bringing their slaves to England. I hope it never will be finally discussed; for I would have all masters think them free and all negroes think they were not, because then they would both behave better.'

Two years after this caution from the bench, the courtroom was once more full of spectators, black and white, eager to learn the judgement in this the latest case. Sharp's only reserve was that West Indian interests had stolen from him the services of the brilliant whig barrister, Dunning, who had defended the slave Lewis so stunningly. So he knew that his opponents' arguments would be propounded by an exceptional advocate. But despite the eloquent pleas of Stewart's legal representatives that: 'The law takes no notice of a negro. Houses, lands, negroes and other real estate may be offered in payment of a a debt,' and their arrogant statement that something that was a possession in Virginia had also to be a possession in London, Lord Chief Justice Mansfield must have realised that in this case he was not going to be able to affirm Stewart's right to his 'property'.

Sharp had hired the services of the barrister Davy to represent Somerset's interests, who refuted his opponents' arguments by saying that the laws of Virginia had no more authority in this country than those of any other foreign country. 'Suppose,' he continued, 'a Turkish pasha come into this country with half a score of Circassian women slaves for his amusement. Suppose they should say to the pasha, "Sir, we will no longer be the subjects of your lust", I believe he would make a miserable figure at the Bar of the Old Bailey on an indictment for rape. I cite the case of Cartwright, who brought a slave from Russia, and would scourge him. For this, he was questioned, and it was resolved that England was too pure an air for slaves to breathe. That was in the eleventh year of the reign of Queen Elizabeth. I hope, my lord, the air does not blow worse since then . . . the moment they set foot on English ground that moment they are free. The case we are presenting here today is that a black is not a thing. And if he is not a thing, he is the King's subject.'

Mansfield was faced with a true dilemma. It was said by the liberals that he delayed so long out of moral cowardice, and by the planters that his final decision was influenced by a negro woman in his household. Both may be partly true but he saw that the laws of property were clear on the side of Stewart, and the laws concerning the rights of the King's subjects were equally clear on the side of Somerset. He knew that his decision would change and influence the law for genera-

49

tions to come, so he delayed. He adjourned the case twice and privately counselled both parties to settle out of court. They refused. He threatened them with the abandonment of the case. They remained unmoved. He urged Stewart to free Somerset, and Sharp to drop the case. Neither party gave any attention to his recommendations. He even tried to suggest that the only solution was to be found in parliamentary legislation. But the protagonists were locked in a struggle which could only be ended by him. 'But if the parties will have it decided,' he wrote, 'we must give an opinion. Compassion will not on the one hand nor inconvenience on the other be to decide, but the law . . . if the parties will have the judgment, *fiat justitia, ruat coelum.*' (Let justice be done, though the heavens fall.)

And so reluctantly, on 22 June, he delivered his long awaited judgement to the packed court. 'The question is,' he began, 'whether the captain has returned a sufficient cause for the detainer of Somerset. The cause returned is, that he had kept him by order of his master, with an intent to send him abroad to Virginia there to be sold. So high an act of dominion must derive its force from the law of the country, and if to be justified here must be justified by the law of England. The state of slavery is of such a nature, that it cannot be introduced on any reasons, moral or political, but only by positive law.' Sharp by now

The tombstone of a slave in Henbury, Bristol. At the time of Lord Mansfield's ruling there were 20,000 slaves in England

Carved figure of a
negro servant,
c. 1800

must have sensed victory. 'It is so odious,' Mansfield continued, 'that nothing can be suffered to support it but positive law. Whatever inconveniences, therefore, may follow from this decision, I cannot say this case is allowed or approved by the law of England. And therefore the black must be discharged.'

Sharp and his followers were overjoyed. And the court echoed with shouts of 'No Property! No Property!' from the blacks who had filled the gallery as they celebrated their victory, the consequences of which neither side could yet appreciate. For Granville Sharp, practically single-handed, had at last set in motion the movement which was to gather such momentum throughout the British Isles that fifty-one years later total abolition of slavery and its attendant trade was ultimately achieved.

For although strictly speaking the judgement found in the Somerset case referred simply to retaining by force the possession of a slave, it had infinitely wider repercussions. For after that date all black slaves in England and Ireland were automatically recognised as free men, and in 1778, with a separate test case of their own, Scotland followed suit. And as well as these all-important legal decisions, there was now also a growing feeling of moral condemnation concerning the business of trading in human beings. Granville Sharp's battle with the judiciary provoked many previously uninterested people into much intensive soul searching. Two of the direct products of this new period of analysis and criticism were a couple of pungent and extremely important attacks on slavery, one by John Wesley who in 1774 published his *Thoughts on Slavery*, and the other by Adam Smith, who argued in his *Wealth of Nations* that the economic justification for slave trading was based on a lie, since the use of slave labour did not pay.

More and more tracts on the subject of slavery were consequently published and the educated English public learnt with some horror the real facts about a system of which prior to this flood of literature they had been practically ignorant. In Philadelphia in 1775 Thomas Paine in his brief tract *African Slavery in America* made the caustic observation that the Americans were busily complaining about the attempts being made to enslave them by Britain while themselves holding literally thousands of Africans in bondage. Promptly one month later the first American Anti-Slavery Society was opened in the town.

The importance of the separation of the thirteen American colonies from the Crown was highly significant. When the War of Independence ended in 1783, the Crown lost the allegiance of the owners of at least 600,000 slaves. It is extremely doubtful that abolition would have been so readily achieved had England still controlled her American Empire. For the slave owners in the south of America were so fervently enamoured of the slave system that they later threatened to separate themselves from the American Republic rather than allow the system to be abolished. It is not difficult to imagine the effect such recalcitrance might have had on the European abolition movement. But the Northern Americas happily were not so firmly wedded to the notion of slavery and the American Quakers, like their English counterparts, outlawed slavery amongst their members very early on and began to take an active part in its very destruction. Many pro-abolitionists were in touch with sympathisers in England, and one of the most influential, Anthony Benezet, published several pamphlets on the subject, which were greatly to change the life of another key figure in the movement, Thomas Clarkson.

This growing use of the published tract and pamphlet was one of the most significant aspects in the fight against slavery. And these publications were not only circulated among the intellectual and political circles, but some even managed to find their way into certain schools. A very large portion of the national conscience was thus being awakened by this stream of intelligent and well-reasoned literature, and thus the published word played an enormously important part in informing and in arming the protagonists for the conflict. And when the War of American Independence was fought and lost by Britain, the moral and intellectual attitudes of many Englishmen underwent a traumatic reappraisal. The loss of the colonies led to a considerable post-war renaissance of thought and attitudes, particularly with regard to what was left of the Empire. India was now the target for British commercial attentions, and the reforms carried out there were largely due to the fact that the loss of America had suddenly made the Eastern continent more economically important. But there were some who took their responsibilities a little less cynically, and these included men like Burke, who espoused the native Indian cause passionately, and others who also believed that the exploitation of primitive people carried heavy moral responsibilities. Humanism was gaining ground. It was even finding its way into politics.

But to the members of the establishment, both during the American war and immediately after it, there was no reason for any change in the hard line they held towards the production of sugar by slave labour. To them there was now an even greater need for sugar colonies and, if possible, for even more of them. And since the great British Navy was now rivalled by the French, the argument that the slave trade was the nursery of seamen was in constant use. Consequently in 1776 and later in 1783 petitions to abolish the slave trade were rejected immediately by both houses. But the difference now was that the supporters of the slave system, for the first time ever, faced an organised and gradually expanding army of intelligent and dedicated opponents. Men who possessed a quickening sense of moral indignation and who shared a common desire to end the traffic and its ancilliary evils. Men like Thomas Clarkson, James Stephen – and William Wilberforce.

53

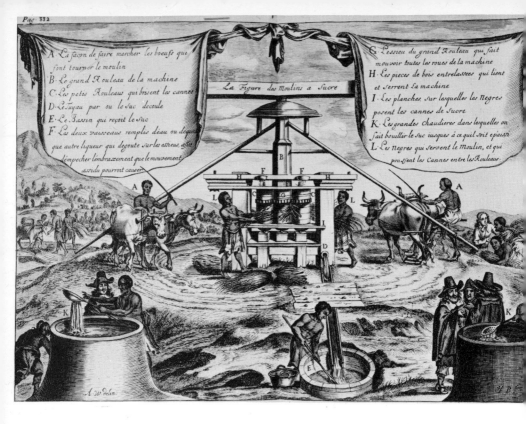

La Figure des Moulins à Sucre

A La façon de faire marcher les boeufs qui font tourner le moulin

B Le grand Rouleau de la machine

C Les petis Rouleaux qui brisent les cannes

D Le Tuyau par ou le Suc decoule

E Le Bassin qui reçoit le Suc

F Les deux vaisseaux remplis d'eau ou de quelque autre liqueur qui degoute sur les essieux, afin d'empecher l'embrazement que le mouvement a'vru du pourroit causer

G L'essieu du grand Rouleau qui fait mouvoir toutes les roues de la machine

H Les pieces de bois entrelassees qui lient et serrent la machine

I Les planches sur lesquelles les Negres posent les cannes de Sucre

K Les grandes chaudieres dans lesquelles on fait bouillir le suc jusques à ce qu'il soit epaissi

L Les Negres qui servent le Moulin, et qui poussent les Cannes entre les Rouleaux

A. W. delin.

Negre domestique aux Isles de l'Amerique coupant des Cannes à Sucre.

Methods of sugar production remained relatively constant for over 250 years as is illustrated by this seventeenth-century engraving (above left) and the photograph which was taken in St Thomas in the early years of this century, and the eighteenth-century sketch and recent photograph of cane cutters

A West Indian plantation
(above right), sugar cane, and
the instruments used in its
cultivation and refinement
(centre right)

The interior of a boiling house
where the juice was boiled and
crystallised (above left). The
sugar, packed in barrels, was
taken to the ports by ox-cart.
This picture is of the Rose Hall
estate

Unloading sugar in Bristol

3. A Matter of Insurance

'Rule Britannia, Britannia rule the waves!
Britons never, never, never shall be slaves!'

(James Thomson. 1740)

At the time of the *Zong* case, which was the next major incident in the
history of the abolition movement, William Wilberforce was still only
twenty-two and but recently elected to Parliament as member for his
native city, Hull. He was the son of a wealthy family, frail and small,
possessing a great gentleness of manner, impish charm, and blessed
with a beautiful singing voice and considerable oratorical gifts. His
best friend was the young William Pitt, who in contrast was tall, aloof
and self-contained, but with the brilliance of mind and dominance of
manner that marked him as a future Prime Minister. Pitt was also in
his early twenties and together they attended balls, dinner parties,
theatres, drinking and gaming parties, indulging in all the pleasures of
eighteenth-century society. Both Wilberforce and Pitt were against
slavery in principle, but neither as yet took an active interest in it, and
Wilberforce, though already interested in religion, had not yet suffered
the profound conversion that was to change the pattern of his life.

In 1781 a certain Luke Collingwood, formerly a ship's surgeon,
accepted the command, his first, of a dilapidated vessel named the
Zong, previously abandoned on the African coast and purchased sight
unseen. He was determined to procure from this, his last intended
slave voyage, sufficient profit to feather the nest of his retirement.
There is no complete record of where he traded, but he may have
landed at Elmina, or any other of the string of fortified trading posts
which stretched for two thousand miles along the coast of Africa. At
these posts, the British, the Portuguese, the Dutch, the French and the
Spaniards had constructed heavily fortified castles, not out of fear of
aggressive Africans, but to protect the claims of these, the maritime
trading nations, against each other. These almost medieval fortress
towns adopted life styles as near to those of their respective homelands
as was possible under the circumstances, being run by a white
governor and officer cadre, and provisioned with imported victuals,
supplemented by locally grown produce. They were a combination of
market place and prison. Slaves were brought in from the interior,

59

sometimes from thousands of miles away, and bartered for manufactured goods. Then they were stored in dungeons until the arrival of
the ships, and resold in large batches to fill the holds of the slavers.

In Collingwood's time, he would have been unlikely to fill his ship
from Elmina or nearby Cape Coast, for the powerful Asante chiefs in
the area had begun to take the trade into their own hands. He would
have bought what he could, and moved on. Like John Newton, thirty
years before, Collingwood may have traded also with small-time
'independent' traders. Though life in the trading fortresses was tedious
and uncomfortable, it was infinitely more luxurious than the lives of
these men, who often lived in unutterable squalor and isolation, in a
climate they found intolerable, with the inevitable consequence that
many died from one of the countless tropical diseases, or from an
addiction to drink brought on by boredom and loneliness. Those who
did survive had only one purpose in mind, to extort as much money
from the system as quickly as possible and retire forthwith to Europe.

It was not difficult for these traders to cheat their homebound employers, as there was little or no way the reported 'losses' of materials
on the Coast could be verified. Their perpetual dishonesty must have
added some spice to the monotonous and uncomfortable daily round.
Few of these men had any interest in the continent that lay around
them, nor in its inhabitants, and it was not until the nineteenth century
that any white man living in Africa was reported as being able to
speak any native dialect. Like those who were afterwards to employ
their live exports in the West Indies, they despised the Africans, and
jeered at the European habits of the self-styled 'kings', failing to
realise that the ragged pantomime costumes of gold braid and faded
uniforms sported by many of these monarchs merely mirrored in a
distorted way the white man's own questionable life style. But it was
the white agents' function to do business with these pantomime figures,
so while they laughed behind their hands, and cheated them with the
shoddy merchandise they used as barter, they still had to keep them
sweet. The African chiefs and traders responded eagerly enough to
their advances, trying desperately to satisfy the ever-growing demand
for slaves in return to brandy, and armaments. 'Give us powder, ball
and brandy,' demanded one chief succinctly. 'In return we have men,
women, and children.'

Collingwood may have moved further west and traded with the
King of Dahomey whose kingdom was built entirely on slavery. The
King had saved his own people merely by making them strong enough
to sell others. Collingwood would have been received in splendid style,
for the King's court, his white plumed hat, his striped silk tents, and

British guests at the annual and bloody ceremony of 'watering the graves of the King's ancestors', from the *History of Dahomey* by Archibald Dalzel who was Governor of Cape Coast Castle in the late eighteenth century

the number of his wives were legendary on the Coast. So was the cruelty of his human sacrifices.

Besides depopulating Africa, exporting her finest and strongest, thus leaving her weak and bewildered, the slave trade corrupted an enormous number of Africans and resulted in a complete degeneration of her culture and art. Local chiefs grew rich from 'dash' and the levy of 'custom duties' (it was possible, as was proved by the King of Wydah, to make £20,000 a year from such dues), and because it became impossible to feed this carniverous cuckoo in their nest, the Africans took to a system of grand pillage, where village would devastate village and tribe massacre tribe.

Conveniently, it was believed in England that the wars which were turning Africa into a battleground were caused by the Africans' natural blood-thirstiness and had nothing to do with slaving. As a contemporary historian put it 'the whole or greater part of that immense continent is a field of warfare and desolation; a wilderness in which the inhabitants are wolves to each other.'

61

Collingwood may have gone even further west, to the Niger delta where the ramshackle town of Calabar grew fat on human misery. It was inhabited by men like Antera Duke, whose pidgin English memoirs of his dealings with slave captains, of wooden houses brought from Liverpool and erected in the Niger mud, of feasting, witchcraft, murder, drunken debauchery and mass decapitation is an unrivalled catalogue of human evil.

The more advanced communities of West Africa had been inland and relatively isolated, trading across the Sahara to the north, and ignoring the Atlantic to the south. The villages on the coast had been the most primitive, mere fishing villages, back doors that led to nowhere. When the slave trade opened those doors, it turned the continent upside down, it despoiled the best of it and enriched the worst.

Certainly, Collingwood stayed too long on the Coast, for by the time he sailed loaded with four hundred slaves his crew was reduced to fourteen men, hardly enough to work the ship, and not enough to allow the slaves on deck for air and exercise. Disease took a heavy toll. His own inexperience as a captain compounded his difficulties, for by a mistake in navigation he sailed past Jamaica, his destination, and was faced with the prospect of a long beat to windward in a leaking ship with an inadequate crew, and a dying cargo. On deck his men were barely strong enough to work the sails, and below in the fetid air of the hold a candle would not burn.

He argued with his mate, Kelsall, that there was not enough water to go around, and that sickness was spreading rapidly. In fact, he feared that if he arrived in Kingston with half his cargo dead, and most of the others sickly, he would not only be blamed but would also lose his percentage of the profit, so having studied well the articles of insurance, he decided to jettison one hundred and thirty-five slaves into the sea, justifying this action by arguing that this was less cruel than 'to suffer them to linger out a few days under the disorders to which they were afflicted.' In due course, the case came up for trial in London, not as a murder case, but as an insurance dispute, since the underwriters had refused to pay the thirty pounds per capita claimed by the owners of the *Zong* for the jettisoned slaves. But the decision went against them, the jury finding 'that the case of slaves was the same as if horses had been thrown overboard.'

The case was brought to the attention of Granville Sharp. Sharp persuaded the underwriters to appeal to a higher court against the decision, and the appeal was heard some months later in the court of the King's Bench, with Sharp's old adversary Lord Mansfield once more presiding. The Solicitor General Lee utterly rejected any appeals to the 'pretended feelings of humanity', asserting the 'unquestionable right of the Master of the vessel to throw overboard as many living slaves as he pleased, providing he exhibited a powerful reason for doing so.' He personally affirmed that there could be no charge of impropriety brought against the captain of the *Zong*. 'What is all this vast declamation about human people being thrown overboard? The question is, was it voluntary or an act of necessity? This is a case of chattels or goods. It is the case of throwing over goods. For to this purpose, and for the purpose of the insurance they are goods and property. This property, human creatures if you will, has been thrown overboard whether or not for the preservation of the rest, that is the real question. Whether right or wrong, we have nothing to do with it.'

Mansfield informed the Solicitor General that the court accepted this contention, but that the point which was to be decided was whether it *was* from necessity. Pigot, representing the underwriters, argued that: 'When the first slaves were thrown overboard, there were on board, three butts of good water. It was therefore only an *apprehended* necessity which is not sufficient. Soon after the rains came which furnished water for eleven days. Notwithstanding which, more of the negroes were thrown overboard.'

To an objection from Lee that there was no evidence of this having happened, Pigot referred him to the transcript of the former trial, which contained the necessary proof. 'The life of one man is like the life of another man,' he continued. 'I contend that as long as any water remained to be divided, those slaves were as much entitled to their share as the captain, the mate or any man whatsoever. I further contend that this loss arose not from the perils of the sea, but from the negligence or ignorance of the captain, for which the owners, and not the insurers, are liable. The truth was that finding that they should have a bad market for their slaves, they took this means of transferring the loss from the owners . . . to the underwriters.'

Mansfield had no option but to find 'that there is great weight in the objection that the evidence does not support the statement of loss made in the declaration. There is weight also in the circumstances of the throwing overboard of the negroes after the rain, for which, upon the evidence, there appears to have been no necessity. There should be . . . on the ground of reconsideration only . . . be a new trial . . . on the payment of costs.'

But a new trial was never held. The crew had dispersed, Collingwood was dead, and Sharp was unable to argue with the accepted interpretation of the law. The only immediate result of the case was a new law, protecting insurance companies against any further claims for slaves thrown overboard. There was not even a suggestion of any proposed legislation to protect or improve the lot of the human cargoes.

By now, there was an obvious need for some concerted effort to be made against the slave trade, so strong was the feeling of hostility towards it growing, and it fell to the Quakers once more to initiate it. In 1783 they formed the committee of six 'for the relief and liberation of the negro slaves in the West Indies, and for the discouragement of the slave trade on the coast of Africa.' The following year they published an anti-slavery tract that was circulated throughout Parliament. But the most important Quaker tract, however, was the one published in 1785 by Benezet on the treatment of slaves in the British colonies. This was greatly to influence and indeed, finally to attract to the movement one of its most tireless campaigners, Thomas Clarkson. But already the Quaker inspired initiative had enabled Sharp to maintain his own inspiration, and even obtain the promises of sympathy and support from some of the bishops. It had also inspired James Ramsay, a clergyman, to devote his entire energies to a series of pamphlets bitterly denouncing slavery.

But it was in Clarkson, the son of a clerical headmaster of a grammar school, that the movement found one of its most exceptional missionaries. The story so far seems already full of miraculous conversions, and moments of divine inspiration. Either the Almighty was more active in those days, or the story of St Paul on the road to Damascus was more popular. At any rate, Thomas Clarkson was no exception to this particular vogue. On the suggestion of his old tutor at Cambridge, he had written and presented an essay entitled 'Is it right to make men slaves against their wills?' Clarkson was delighted to win first prize, and might then have let the matter rest but on his way back to London the problems he had discussed in his paper began to weigh heavily upon him, and he started to examine the implications of slavery. '. . . all my pleasure was damped by the facts which were now continually before me. In the daytime, I was uneasy. In the night I had little rest. I sometimes never closed my eyes for grief . . . I frequently tried to persuade myself that the contents of my essay could not be true . . . coming in sight of Wades Mill in Hertfordshire, I sat down disconsolate on the turf by the road side, and held my horse . . . here a thought came into my mind, that if the contents were true, it was time some person should see these calamities to their end.'

Clarkson was very different in character from Granville Sharp and William Wilberforce. Sharp was musical, brilliant, and more than slightly eccentric, towards the end of his life becoming totally obsessed with interpreting the prophecies in the books of David and Revelations. Wilberforce was a magnetic, lyrical sprite. Clarkson was a worthy but stuffy pedant. Sarah Fox described him as being 'obsessed with the weight of good work' and his writings on the subject of slavery certainly affirm this slightly sanctimonious quality. But it was this very thorough and stolid approach to the problem that enabled Clarkson to seek the truth with such utter dedication, for although

Thomas Clarkson in 1798 by C. F. Von Breda

given to the pursuit of the occasional red herring, he was not a man to be deterred by threats, hostilities, or even, as on one occasion, an attempt on his life. Never a rich man, he became so involved in the conflict that he impoverished himself even further during the time he spent trailing round the ports of England and assimilating all the vital information. So when Clarkson finally retired, in 1794, Wilberforce had to organise an annuity for him, which philanthropic move was fortunately successful enough to establish Clarkson as a farmer in the Lake District.

65

Immediately after Clarkson arrived in London he joined the then thin ranks of the abolitionists through meetings with Sharp, Ramsay and Dillwyn, and in 1787 the committee of twelve was formed whose nucleus was the earlier Quaker committee of 1783. Clarkson published his Latin essay in order to reach a larger audience, and the committee began a pamphleteering campaign with the object of disseminating their arguments to as large an audience as possible. But paper propaganda alone was inadequate, and the search was on for a leader who could give power, respectability and inspiration to the movement. The House of Commons was largely indifferent, and in some instances openly hostile to any suggestion of abolishing a trade upon which such a massive part of England's blossoming economy depended, and

William
Wilberforce
in 1828 by
Sir Thomas
Lawrence

furthermore any of the liberal or crusading politicians who privately subscribed to the belief that the trade was immoral and unsupportable were afraid to espouse the cause openly in the House for fear of upsetting the delicate political balance within their respective parties. Burke, an ardent humanist and champion of the oppressed, sat on his 1780 Bill for twelve years due to party pressures, for he feared such a crusade would split the Whigs, and ruin any chance of achieving a successful abolition of the trade. Pitt was in exactly the same position with the Tories, and to make the matter even more complicated, the West Indian interests were more than adequately represented in Parliament by members elected from boroughs which had been 'bought' by the planters. So it was a formidable task for anybody to undertake, and there certainly seemed to be no politician of the time sufficiently uncommitted to have stepped out of line and won the right to make the abolition of the slave trade a government measure. Or so it appeared until Pitt pressed his young contemporary William Wilberforce to pick up the torch, and the abolition movement gained its most famous advocate.

It is very much the style of the age in which we now live to suspect the heroes of the past. For up until recently there was still a general belief that the British inheritance was one of benificence towards backward and oppressed people, and that the national pride was based on philanthropy rather than vainglorious Imperialism. Now that we are going through an intense period of self-appraisal, which naturally affects our previous historical attitudes, we no longer see a man such as William Wilberforce as the haloed saint, labouring selflessly for the liberation of the unfortunate negro, at the head of his devoted band, but possibly as a man who took advantage of his moment, and who finally, by dint of his equivocal attitude, actually prolonged the misery of slavery.

As is usually the case, the truth lies somewhere between these two extremes. William Wilberforce certainly confessed to the fact that his own distinction was 'his darling object', and before his religious conversion, he seemed as committed to enjoying the high life as were most of his contemporaries. His company was widely sought, and even as a young man his opponents were already uncommonly jealous of him. But perhaps it was his conversion that many of his contemporaries found hardest to stomach, and that many modern historians still do. For after he had travelled to France in the company of an old teacher, Isaac Milner, Wilberforce shut himself away from all his worldly pursuits, resigning his club and declining all invitations as he underwent this period of philosophical and religious reappraisal. Though he had been interested in religion as a child, his mature 'conversion' was initiated by Milner, strengthened by thought and study, and finally consolidated through dialogue with the formidable Reverend Newton. Wilberforce emerged as a totally changed man, and although this heartily saddened his closest friend, and fellow drinking companion, Pitt, it also provided the abolition movement with its ideal leader. For Wilberforce was no longer interested in parliamentary promotion, so as a cross-bencher he was perfectly suited to bearing the banner, unaffected by the pressures of political life. And sickening as it may have seemed to his enemies, his aura of sanctity and holiness elevated him well above the ranks of the ordinary jobbing politicians.

There are inevitably sharp contradictions in Wilberforce's life, and unfortunately the critics of the famous always make great capital from such paradoxes. His worst fault seems to have been that while he fought all his life for the improvement in the lot of slaves abroad, he was a thoroughgoing conservative at home supporting the Corn Laws and the Suppression Acts, and substituting charity for crusade when dealing with the English working class. This led to his enemies accusing him of hypocrisy and equivocation, and of possessing an unseemly desire to play safe, and thus be accepted by all. Certainly he was sufficiently canny never to find himself outlawed by the society in which he enjoyed moving. He managed to advocate the benefits of Christianity to primitive people, and criticise the immorality of the slave trade without ever unduly upsetting the clergy, and was politically adroit enough to remain an independent without alienating either of the opposing parties. But although skilful at self-manipulation within the political and social circles, in his time he attracted a tremendous amount of hostility and came in for a variety of highly caustic assaults. 'Mr Wilberforce,' said Hazlitt in an essay on 'The Spirit of the Age', 'is far from being a hypocrite, but he is we think as fine a specimen of moral equivocation as can well be conceived.' And his old crusader, Thomas Clarkson, was moved to complain to Coleridge after Wilberforce had died that 'He cared nothing about the slaves, not if they were all damned, provided he saved his own soul.'

Perhaps it was the aura of divine self-righteousness that surrounded Wilberforce that irritated his contemporaries. And if it was hard for them to accept it, it is even more difficult for commentators living in this atheistic age. But it is important if we are to understand his character to view him in the light of the then prevalent religious atmosphere. For in the middle of the eighteenth century there was a tremendous Evangelical movement which influenced and enmeshed a great many rational and thoughtful people. Conversion usually produced not necessarily a better balanced person, but usually a rather pious and devoted crusader, a person easily shocked by injustice and perfidy, but assured in a belief in the Divine Order of All Things. And whereas many were thus inspired to campaign and fight the evils of the slave trade, this Evangelical spirit also unfortunately led to the patronisingly superior attitude adopted by the Christian white over pagan black.

Even when he was alive Wilberforce was subjected to much criticism and ridicule because of his godliness and to constant suspicion because of his seemingly contradictory behaviour. But he would have earned his place in history just for the fact that he was there to undertake the fight at the right time and for most of the right reasons. If Wilberforce had not organised the campaigning and lent his considerable political reputation to the movement when he did, it is impossible to surmise what might, or probably more correctly, what might not have happened. His presence lent that essential magic and inspiration to the enterprise, and although later the society was to be spoilt by dissension and rancour in its second generation, it might never even have got as far as a second generation had not Wilberforce agreed to Pitt's proposal that he should give notice to Parliament of an intention to bring in a motion on the subject of the slave trade. It was a subject perfectly suited to Wilberforce's new found idealism, and having made some tentative requests for information he was already partially involved. As they sat together picnicking overlooking the Vale of Keston on that historic day, Pitt warned Wilberforce that he would be taking on vast commercially vested interests and 'all the bigotry and ignorance with which our country is so generously endowed,' and that although he, Pitt, would support him fully, it could only be proposed as a private not as a government motion. But to Wilberforce the offer must have seemed providential, and he therefore found little difficulty in accepting the task, a decision that was to have massive repercussions, some of which still echo around our modern world.

From a map of Sierra Leone in C. D. Wadstrom's *Essays on Colonization* (1794) — a guide for would-be immigrants to the new British West African colonies

4. Tight Packers and Loose Packers

'Captain Crow da come again . . .
Wit him hearty, joyful gay.'

In 1787, Thomas Clarkson, with the backing of Wilberforce and the Abolition Committee set off on the first of his epic journeys to the ports of England to investigate the slave trade. Wilberforce and his friends realised that horror stories and moral condemnation would never achieve the end of the slave system, facts were necessary, meticulously researched and carefully presented, facts and alternatives. So from this time on the abolitionists began to piece together an alternative policy based on commerce, Christianity and culture. What we would now decry as colonialism was at that time both radical and humane.

They had already started the beginnings of their missionary activities which were later to be consolidated into more permanent forms with the foundation of the Church Missionary Society in 1799, the British and Foreign Bible Society in 1804, and the easier admission of missionaries to India in 1813. Also many of the abolitionists were beginning to propose the perfectly feasible alternative of a 'legitimate' trade between Africa and England based on the exchange of the foreign goods the chiefs wanted for native but inanimate African produce, in the hope that the slave trade would thus be ousted and die a natural death.

But the most dramatic example of this new policy was the idea of sending the black poor back to Africa. Mansfield's historic judgment in the Somerset case had released some twenty thousand slaves into the streets of English cities. They found little employment and less charity. A certain Dr Sweatman suggested to Granville Sharp that they might be transported back to Africa. Sharp saw in the idea the opportunity to put the new policy into practice and he promoted it with his customary enthusiasm. Africa would be colonised by her own people in a properly organised community dedicated to legitimate trade and ruled by Christian principles.

The colony of Sierra Leone was founded by three groups of settlers under the sponsorship of a private company of which Sharp and Wilberforce were directors. The first group was a party of 450 negroes accompanied by 60 white women from the slums of London who arrived in 1787 and named their first settlement Granville Town in honour of Sharp. They were joined in 1792 by 1000 blacks who had espoused the British cause in the American War of Independence and had taken refuge in Nova Scotia. The third group were Maroons who had revolted against slavery in Jamaica, and had held out in the mountain fastnesses for a hundred years. Under a peace treaty signed with the British in 1796 many were deported to Nova Scotia, and requesting transfer to Africa arrived in Sierra Leone in 1800.

The early years of the colony is a tale of death and of disaster. The project, full of well-intentioned enthusiasm, was ill-planned, many died on the voyages, or succumbed on arrival to tropical diseases. The local tribes were hostile to the invasion, and almost wiped out the colony in 1789. Their supply ships were sunk or captured in the Napoleonic wars, and in 1794 the French navy destroyed the new settlement at Freetown. Food was always in short supply and there was dissension among the different groups of pioneers. That they survived is due in part to the efforts of Zachary Macaulay, their first governor, an abolitionist, and father of the famous Whig historian, Thomas Macaulay. In 1807 though only half of the original 3000 settlers were left alive, the infant colony was adopted by the Crown and passed into the protection and control of the British government. Today it is the independent state of Sierra Leone.

The history of the colony can be read either as an abolitionist success, a story of black heroism, or even as an early example of the 'high-handed and arrogant' policy adopted towards the blacks by the abolitionists and later by British colonialists. Certainly it is possible that the majority of abolitionists believed in 'uplifting' the negro rather than in liberating him, and Wilberforce himself in his *Appeal in Behalf of the Negro Slaves in the West Indies* considered the moral and religious degradation of the slaves with more horror than the punishments, tortures and barbarities which were constantly inflicted upon them, and assured his readers that they should 'raise these poor creatures from their depressed condition, and if they are not yet fit for the enjoyment of British freedom, elevate them at least from the level of the brute creation into that of rational creatures . . . taught by Christianity, they will sustain with patience the sufferings of their actual lot, while the same instructors will rapidly prepare them for a better; and instead of being objects at one time of contempt, and another of terror, they will soon be regarded as a grateful peasantry.'

Naturally the modern mind is inclined to baulk at such a sanctimonious philosophy, and place much of the blame for our present

Zachary
Macaulay
by F. Slater,
and the
coinage of
the Sierra
Leone colony

racial troubles on the shoulders of these so-called 'enlightened' do-gooders, suspecting them of being rascists in liberal clothing. But whatever legacy of disorder we have inherited as a direct or indirect result of their 'misplaced' humanism, it must be remembered that in their proper historical context, these reformers were as daring and as outspoken as many of the present-day militants. However, many of the best-intentioned of them were propertied men who, therefore, respected the ownership of property and according to Wilberforce, treated 'with candour and tenderness the characters of the West India proprietors.' But this should make their humanitarianism no more suspicious than that of a well-intentioned trade union leader who believes wholeheartedly in the sanctity of the working class. It is perhaps preferable to judge these zealots on their actual achievements rather than blame them for the mistakes enacted by others after them. And these men and women, however sugary their piety, and however sanctimonious their philosophy, stepped out of line and at considerable risk to themselves, to attack the mainstay of their country's economic prosperity.

Thomas Clarkson, as he set out on his investigation, realised with some trepidation what he was about to undertake. 'I begin now to tremble for the first time,' he wrote, 'at this arduous task I have undertaken, attempting to subvert the commerce of the great place which is now before me. I anticipate much persecution . . . and I question whether I shall even get out of it alive.'

His fears were well founded. For here was a young man, armed only with a notebook and pencil, whose intention it was to invade the docklands of Bristol, London and Liverpool to collect the evidence he needed to destroy their very wealth. It was not surprising that he met with intense hostility and threats of violence; what was surprising was that he survived at all, for these great ports had flourished from the profits of the triangular trade, and in Liverpool not only did the city itself depend on this commerce, but the areas immediately surrounding the Mersey were rapidly enriching themselves by supplying the necessary raw materials. Manchester was said by Sir John Chapman to 'live on shirts made from black men.' The millhands in distant Sheffield, and shipbuilders, gunsmiths and sail-makers working in the vicinity of the ports all thrived on this rapidly expanding trade. Liverpool in the mid-eighteenth century was a seaside village. By 1800 it was the leading slave port, averaging over eighty triangular trips each year, and drawing a yearly income of over one million pounds. Everybody in the city profited from the trade, from the humblest grocer to the richest banker.

The Abolition Committee had by now firmly declared its policy, namely to attack the trade solely, and not the actual practice of slavery. As Clarkson later noted: 'It was of consequence which of the two evils the committee was to select as the object for their labours. It appeared soon to be the sense of the committee that to aim at the removal of both would be to aim at too much, and that by doing this we might lose all.'

There was little disagreement with such a 'reasonable' policy. It did not appear to be unduly inflammatory, there was little danger of subsequent revolution if successfully carried out, and there were benefits to be reaped for all. For by abolishing the iniquitous trade which was rapidly earning the disapproval of all sensible people, the owners of the plantations, realising that their slaves could not be replaced, would be forced to treat them with greater respect, to encourage them to breed by promising them better conditions, and to educate them in readiness for a Christian conversion.

Clarkson appeared to subscribe wholeheartedly to this absurdly idealistic belief, assuring the readers of his pamphlets, that the planters would build up stocks of healthy slaves, and that the slaves thus bred on the plantations under these conditions, would be 'united from their infancy to labour.'

However absurd in theory he was precise in his investigations. In Liverpool he visited a slave ship lying at anchor. 'I found myself for the first time on the deck of a slave-vessel. The sight of the rooms below and of the gratings above, and of the barricado across the deck, and the explanation of all these, filled me both with melancholy and horror. I soon found afterwards a fire of indignation kindle within me.'

His indignation grew stronger when he saw in an ironmonger's shop all the instruments of torture that were used on the slaves, the shackles and fetters, the whips, iron collars, thumbscrews and forced feeders that were the standard equipment of the Guineamen. Furthermore he interviewed surgeons and travellers who had worked them, in order to doublecheck all his facts. He was a tireless and energetic detective, riding on horseback for literally thousands of miles in a matter of months in order to gather his material, and refusing to be intimidated by any of the threats against him. It was a formidable task, but fortunately he was blessed with that particularly bull-necked type of determination which is not deterred by scaremongering. He was once nearly murdered. Alone on a wharf in Liverpool, he was surrounded by a gang of sailors, one of whom had been pointed out to him as the murderer of a shipmate, and who obviously now intended to murder

Clarkson and throw him into the sea. But Clarkson with great presence of mind put his head down and charged them, and being a large man, dispersed them with this surprise tactic. He was back on the docks the next day collecting more evidence.

Following the agreement made with Wilberforce, and in accordance with the policy of the abolitionists, Clarkson now devoted all his time to collecting evidence about the lot of the sailors, which would enable him to present a damning indictment of a trade that so brutalised and debased its employees. He researched and documented many reports of sailors being flogged to death for the most trivial of misdemeanours, and discovered other cases of murder and torture on board these so-called 'nursery' ships. He unearthed the murder of one sailor who had his brains beaten out with the end of a heavily knotted rope, and the torture of another who had hot pitch poured into wounds on his back. Flogging spread like a contagion in certain vessels, captains often ordering it purely as a distraction from boredom, while the day-to-day conditions the sailors had to endure at sea were often indescribable. Their rations were a pound of bread and a pound of salt beef a day, a drink of water was often completely impossible to come by, crippling diseases such as scurvy and opthalmia were commonplace, while the infections picked up from the African slaves in the holds further decimated their numbers. And because the dreadful reputations of the Guineamen began to precede them, it became increasingly difficult to recruit crews for them, with the consequence, as Clarkson noted, that the conditions ashore at the slaving ports often became as dangerous as those at sea. 'Music, dancing, rioting, drunkenness and profane swearing were kept up from night to night. The young mariner, if a stranger to a port, and unacquainted with the nature of the slave trade was certain to be picked up. The novelty of the voyages, the superiority of the wages in this over any other trades, and the privileges of various kinds were set before him . . . if these prospects did not attract him, he was plied with liquor until he became intoxicated when a bargain was made over him between the landlord and the mate.'

Or he might just simply be knocked out in a dark alley behind the tavern and carried still unconscious aboard a Guineaman lying at anchor off the coast. Once aboard there was no redress.

So involved did Clarkson become with their fortunes, that he traced the histories of at least twenty thousand sailors. His dogged persistence became legendary, with the unfortunate result that his reputation began to precede him, and those who might have been willing to talk to him often went to ground. Ships doctors whom he interviewed were subsequently refused sea trips, tradesmen who co-operated had their

Liverpool in the early nineteenth century.
During this period its most rapid growth was largely financed by slavery

A model, belonging to Wilberforce, of a slave ship

Thomas Clarkson by A. E. Chalon, with some of the goods he collected to prove the viability of regular trade with Africa

businesses boycotted; witnesses would suddenly change their minds or just disappear altogether. Sometimes, when he was fortunate enough to find willing witnesses, Clarkson found it hard to believe some of the facts. He once heard of an intention to sail to Africa a vessel which had been built as a river pleasure craft. The ship was designed to carry six people, and its hold was only thirty-one feet long and two and a half feet high. The slaves were to be stowed below like sacks of corn, one on top of another. Suspecting a ploy to discredit him, he checked and doublechecked until he discovered it was true, and that this preposterous undertaking was indeed seriously intended.

What had started out in Clarkson's mind as an examination of the general conditions of the slave trade, had now turned into a burning crusade against the conditions for men serving on these terrible ships. He had, however, also found time to make a collection of native African produce which he intended to use to back up his argument for a 'legitimate' trade. He returned to London in a state of high agitation, armed with an almost encyclopedic amount of evidence, and with a collection of African handiwork, gold and silver jewellery, leather goods, ivory, palm oil and lengths of woven cloth.

Wilberforce had not been idle either. Since agreeing to lead the abolition movement, he had spent the months reading everything he could about the slave trade, and had spent hours arguing with his friend Pitt on the best approach they could take in order to satisfy their mutual ambition. Pitt was, as always, staunchly opposed to a continuance of the trade, but as Prime Minister he found it impossible to make it the major issue on his parliamentary agenda. He met Clarkson at Wilberforce's suggestion, and argued that he could not give abolition priority over other more pressing concerns, such as the trouble in the Low Countries, the state of the King's health, the Question of Reform, and the Irish situation. 'And if you were Prime Minister,' he asked 'would you not leave well alone an enterprise on which the nation thrives?'

'It thrives to the damnation of us all,' Clarkson replied. Pitt then attempted to convince him of the political difficulties, indicating the stubborn opposition he would meet from his Lord Chancellor, Lord Thurlow, and from Sydney, his Secretary of State. But Clarkson's agitation was intense, and was not to be cooled by the posturing of politicians, and in answer to the argument that the self-interest of the merchants and the slave captains was a guarantee of the slaves' safe conduct, Clarkson explained the theory of 'tight and loose packing'. If a ship carried only one hundred slaves and they all survived the journey the cargo would be worth approximately £5000, while if the same ship carried five hundred and delivered four hundred alive, the cargo was worth £20,000. Nor did Clarkson subscribe to the belief that unless England persuaded France to abolish at the same time she would make a gift of her commerce to her enemy, particularly since he proposed to establish legitimate trade in its place. Pitt was impressed by Clarkson's missionary zeal and by the facts he was presenting to back up his arguments, in particular the figures he quoted from the muster-rolls, which verified the high death rate and desertion rates among the British crews on the slave ships. In 1787, 88 ships had cleared from Liverpool for Africa, with 3170 sailors, of which 642 died, 1100 deserted in Africa or the West Indies, and 1428, less than half, returned. Although Pitt was still unable to commit his party or his government, he ordered the Trade Committee of the Privy Council to make an enquiry into and submit a report on the slave trade, and instructed the British Ambassador in Paris to test opinion for a possible joint attempt at abolition. The latter venture was doomed from the start, for the French refused to commit themselves, and thus no guarantee could be ventured as to the safety of British commercial interests. For unlike Thomas Clarkson, Parliament did not believe that France would be swayed by the moral force of England's example.

Pitt, however, was determined to press on for abolition, despite the growing difficulties and the possible commercial disadvantages. And when Wilberforce fell dangerously ill early in 1788, and it seemed probable that the movement would lose its leader, Pitt promised he would take on the leadership in Parliament, and in May he moved a resolution binding the House to an examination of the slave trade when the Privy Council had finished its enquiry. The passing of this resolution with no opposition was hardly an enormous landmark in the fight against slavery, but it did illustrate a slight shift in the attitude of the House, and before this particular parliamentary session closed, a Bill, introduced by Sir William Dolben, was actually passed which proposed to limit the amount of slaves carried per ship according to tonnage. All the supporters of the slave trade at once showed themselves in their true colours, minimising the horrors of the Middle Passage, and protesting that any interference with the trade would ruin it. Pitt, in answer to their protests, threatened immediate and entire abolition if they did not give their assent to this Bill, which unsurprisingly led to it being passed with an overwhelming majority.

As for the Privy Council, although some of the testimony was obviously blatant perjury, its report published just over a year after it was convened was the most important document to be published so far. For although it took no stand on the morality of slavery, its massive compilation of evidence, carefully reported and edited, with the sanction of Parliament made it an invaluable reference book for the abolitionists. It dealt, in carefully divided categories, with every aspect of the slave trade, and although some aspects were more fully researched and documented than others, much hitherto unpublished evidence was brought to light by its proceedings. Firstly it covered the position of the African in his own homeland, but of course since little was known about native Africa, most of the evidence offered to the council only supported the prevalent ignorant attitudes, namely that the blacks had no 'proper' religion, and were totally without any moral scruples, although the odd voice was occasionally heard to state that it was only those blacks who had come into contact with the white men who had become corrupted.

The aged Rev. John Newton gave touching testimony. He was asked, 'What was the opinion entertained of the Europeans, in your time, by the natives of the part of Africa in which you lived?' Newton replied, 'There were individuals thought well of by the natives, but they had no good opinion of them upon the whole; and sometimes when charged with a fraud or crime, would say, "What, do you think I am a white man?" '

But most of the evidence given was a vindication of the traders' arguments that those exported to the West Indies as slaves were those men who were already enslaved within their own tribes for criminal misdemeanours, this belief also justifying the barbarous laws later imposed on the slaves when they reached the colonies. Many also believed that the transference of these poor wretches from their uncivilised country to the Christian paradise of the West Indies was indeed their salvation.

In its report on the evidence dealing with the Middle Passage the report is at its most dramatic and controversial. This aspect of the triangular trade was always the most notorious, so naturally horrific stories and contradictory ones abounded. Captain Crow, one of the most famous and controversial slave captains, gave evidence of how he fed his 'passengers' on large quantities of dried shrimp, served on a bed of rice and beans, and generally tended to their daily requisites with great concern. 'They come on deck at eight o'clock, and they are provided with water to wash, lime juice and chew sticks for cleaning their teeth. There is a dram of brandy bitters for each of the men, and then with clean spoons being served out, they breakfast at nine . . . at eleven they wash their bodies, and anoint themselves with palm oil, their favourite cosmetic. Meanwhile their apartments are purified with frankincense and lime juice . . . then a midday mess of bread and coconuts, and the main meal at three o'clock. In the evening, song and dance are promoted. The men are permitted to play and sing, while the women make fanciful ornaments with their beads . . . [the sick] are given nourishing soups made of mutton, goats or chickens, to which is added sago and lillipees, and the whole flavoured with port and wine and sugar . . . Nothing is spared that might contribute to their personal comfort . . . when I arrive in Jamaica, do you know, I am welcomed by the blacks, who have travelled with me.'

Such evidence contrasted rather whimsically with the sworn reports of the mass poisoning, rape and murder of the slaves as reported by slightly more reliable witnesses such as Dr Alexander Falconbridge, a

Captain Crow, and his ship *Ceres* (damaged after a storm) on the final lap of its triangular course carrying sugar and coffee

ship's surgeon who had served aboard the Guineamen. He told the council that when trade was slack on the Coast, the captain of a certain Bristol slaver 'would fire his guns into the town to freshen them up a bit.' As for the slaves once stowed away in the holds 'they had not so much room as a man in his coffin, either in length or breadth.' When he had to enter the slave deck he took off his shoes 'to avoid crushing the slaves as he was forced to crawl over them.' He further added he still had 'the marks on his feet where [the slaves] bit and pinched him.'

'I recall a woman we had taken on board the *Alexander* . . . she was taken ill of a dysentery and would take neither food or medicines. I often tried to make her swallow wine, but never could. I desired the interpreter to ask her what she wanted . . . she wanted nothing but to die . . . and she did die . . . I once saw a pregnant woman give birth to her baby while still shackled to a corpse that our drunken overseer had neglected to remove . . . For the purpose of admitting fresh air most of the ships in the slave trade are provided, between the decks, with five or six air ports on each side of the ship, about six inches in length and four in breadth . . . but whenever the sea is rough and the rain heavy, it becomes necessary to shut these and every other conveyance by which the air is admitted . . . the negroes' rooms very soon become intolerably hot, the confined air rendered noxious by the effluvia exhaled from their bodies and by being repeatedly breathed, soon produces

fevers and fluxes which generally carry off great numbers of them.'

While the council was still sifting the evidence, Clarkson became very depressed at the way events were shaping. There seemed to be no end of powerful men willing to perjure themselves for the sake of their wealth, and whenever the abolitionists won a concession, immediately some establishment figure, such as Admiral Rodney, would testify and plead the safety of the nation. Admiral Rodney assured the Privy Council that he had seen no instances of any cruelty in the West Indian plantations, that the slaves were better fed than the British labouring community, and that after an enjoyable day in the fields the slaves danced and made merry. He solemnly warned the council

83

members if the British slave trade were abolished 'it would add greatly to the naval power of France and diminish that of Great Britain in proportion.' Clarkson was also losing faith in Pitt and informed Wilberforce (who was making a miraculous recovery from his near fatal illness, largely helped by the properties of the drug opium), that he would prefer reliance on Fox rather than the Prime Minister. Wilberforce naturally defended his personal friend and parliamentary ally, and tried to dissuade Clarkson from his headstrong plans for holding public meetings and a march on Parliament. This division of opinion over the most effective mode of action was later to split the Abolition Society into two strongly opposed schools of thought, one favouring Wilberforce's more orthodox and conservative approach, the other a much more militant plan of action. But at this time there was no severe breach between Clarkson and Wilberforce, even though some abolitionists were beginning to suspect their leader of having too many friends who were themselves slave-owners.

Since great emphasis was being placed on the claim that in Africa the trade was natural and accepted, and that there was no forcible abduction or kidnapping, Clarkson and Wilberforce decided to try and find an eye-witness who could discredit this claim by giving evidence about the actual methods of capturing slaves. Clarkson, after visiting forty-six ships, finally tracked down a sailor named Isaac Parker who he had heard would be willing to talk. Parker gave evidence to the council, testifying that it was standard practice to mount armed raids up river in order to capture unsuspecting natives, and that he himself with Dick Ebro, an African trader, had sailed on such an expedition when they had captured a band of men, women and children. This evidence, backed up by that of witnesses like the explorer Dr Spaarman (who testified how he witnessed a drunken native 'king' short of brandy, sending out a new party to collect slaves), was sufficiently damning.

The other parts of the Privy Council report dealt with the treatment of the slaves in the plantations, the extent of the trade, the success of the French Colonies, and the trade of Britain's rivals with Africa. It was impossible for the abolitionists to present any evidence against the theory that the slave trade was all-important to Britain's economic health, and it was this obstacle which was to prove one of their greatest stumbling blocks. But they got an unexpected bonus in the council's report when they published their findings on an examination of the slave laws imposed in the colonies. That they were so impersonal and horrific (once more based on the tenet that slaves were mere property), was shocking enough. What appalled the public even more was the fact that these vicious laws were a product of the British statute book. And although the publication of the report in no way led to any direct or tangible consequence it became a very important weapon in the growing propaganda warfare.

The most immediate result of its publication was the determination of Wilberforce, now fully recovered, to force the issue in the House of Commons. He considered the report had supplied sufficient facts about the trade for him to demand its total abolition, and on 12 May 1789 he rose to deliver a brilliant three-hour speech which Burke was later to compare with 'the remains of Grecian eloquence'.

'The nature and all the circumstances of this trade are now laid open to us,' he began, 'we can no longer plead ignorance . . . I wish exceedingly, at the outset, to guard both myself and the House from entering into the subject with any sort of passion. I ask only for your impartial reason . . . I mean to take the shame upon myself in common with the whole parliament of Great Britain for having suffered this horrid trade to be carried on under our authority. We are all guilty. We ought to plead guilty, and not to excuse ourselves by throwing the blame on others.'

He then dealt with how the trade affected Africa, trying to find an explanation for the reported barbarity of the natives. 'With a country vast in its extent, not utterly barbarous, but civilised in a very small degree, does anyone suppose a slave trade would help their civilisation? Is it not plain that she must suffer from it; that her civilisation must be checked; her barbarous manners made more barbarous? . . . Does not everyone see that a slave trade carried on around the coasts of Africa must carry violence and desolation to its very centre? The vices of avarice and sensuality, we tempt, we stimulate, in all the African princes. Does the king want brandy? He has only to send his troops to burn and desolate a village for the captives will serve as commodity to barter with a British trader. It is a trade calculated to spread disunion, to inspire enmity, and to destroy humanity.'

Wilberforce then continued by refuting the whimsical evidence about the Middle Passage given by certain witnesses in front of the Privy Council, and asked the House to consider the stark facts as sufficient proof.

'Death is at least a sure ground of proof. It will be found from the evidence given at the Privy Council that not less than $12\frac{1}{2}\%$ perish during the passage. Not less than $4\frac{1}{2}\%$ die on shore before the time of their sale. And one third more die in the seasoning. Upon the whole there is a mortality of about 50%, and this among negroes who are not bought unless as the phrase is with cattle, they are sound in wind and

William Pitt, addressing the Commons as Prime Minister in 1793, by Karl Anton Hickel. Wilberforce is seated in front of the right-hand pillar and Charles Fox is sixth from the right in the front row

limb. What need is there for further testimony? The number of deaths speaks for itself, and makes all inquiry superfluous.'

He ended his first great speech on abolition with the proposition which was to gain great favour as the campaign matured.

'Let us make a reparation to Africa so far as we can by establishing a trade upon the commercial principles, and we shall soon find the rectitude of our conduct rewarded by the benefits of a regular and growing commerce.'

When Wilberforce finally sat down at the end of his historic speech, he may have sensed victory, for the opposition was disorganised and its speeches largely composed of bland fatuities, while he was ably supported by orators such as Burke and Fox. Burke argued that if any trade or commerce was lost as a consequence of abolition it would not be sufficient to justify 'the old plea of necessity'. 'And besides,' he added, 'are we not prepared to pay the price of virtue?'

Fox pleaded 'If we do not by our votes tonight mark to all mankind our abhorrence of a practice so enormous, so savage, so repugnant to all laws human and divine, it will be more scandalous in the eyes of the country and the world than any vote which the House of Commons has ever given. If we vote that the slave trade should not be abolished we give a parliamentary sanction to rapine, robbery and murder; for a system of rapine, robbery, and murder the slave trade has now clearly proved to be.'

This was powerful oratory, particularly when contrasted with the level of schoolboy debate offered by the opposition. Grosvenor, while agreeing that the slave trade was not an 'amiable' trade, argued that neither was butchery, 'yet a mutton chop is a very good thing . . . You have all heard of the haberdasher's wife who locked the apprentice girl in the cupboard and starved her to death, but did anybody ever think of abolishing haberdashery on that account?'

This was about the standard of their argument, backed up by predictable but dubious proprietorial claims concerning 'property' and 'gentleman planters' rights'. Listening to this feeble and arrogant opposition, Wilberforce must have felt that an early and perhaps even overwhelming victory was imminent. But such hopes were premature, and were about to be sadly dashed. For the House, although it had listened attentively to the debate, was still much confused about the matter, its conscience being, as Coupland puts it, in 'conflict with [its] native caution.' This is a somewhat generous interpretation of the decision reached by the House. It would be fairer to accuse it of cowardice, for it was much too concerned with self-interest, and the protection of the profitable commerce which resulted directly from the slave trade. So although the good men and the star performers in the House had aligned themselves with the cause, it was the 'minor orators, the dwarfs, and the pigmies' who carried the vote against the proposal, and it was defeated by 163 to 88.

So the first great campaign ended in failure; but the abolitionists were not deterred, and in fact this set-back only spurred them to even more furious activity, which led to a massive mobilisation of public opinion. England was gripped by abolitionist fever which swept the country and prompted Lord Thurlow to remark caustically that it was only a 'five days' fit of philanthropy'. But the hostility of the unenlightened barely covered their very real fear, occasioned by the frenzy which was gripping the people of England. The Abolition Society was becoming highly skilled at organising propaganda warfare, and the system they evolved has acted since as a blueprint for revolutionary organisations. Basically they created a series of committees set up throughout the country which would both disseminate information and also organise local opinion. Their tireless workers, both men and women (although Wilberforce took great exception to the presence of the latter within the Society), travelled the length and breadth of the country on exhausting tours to keep the public informed of the latest developments. The main committee met ceaselessly to organise the campaign and the distribution of material, and in one year printed over 25,000 reports and nearly 50,000 pamphlets and essays, including Clarkson's *Summary View of the Slave Trade*, Newton's *Thoughts* and *Equiano's Travels*, which by 1827 had gone through seventeen editions. Olaudah Equiano was captured as a boy and sold as a slave. He later became famous as one of the first African authors. He was stolen, aged only ten, from his Ibo village which lay deep inland, and sold into a slave coffle headed for the coast. Transported to the West Indies, he was sold to the master of a small vessel trading among the islands, and later to a family in the American south. Self-taught, he became a clerk, saved enough money to buy his freedom, and became a professional sailor. He visited the Mediterranean, and went on an expedition to the Arctic in 1773. In 1789, he published his book. As an ardent member of the anti-slavery movement, he knew and influenced the leading English abolitionists. He married an Englishwoman, and died in London in 1797.

The Abolition Society initiated a system of sanctions against West Indian grown sugar, which was popularly known as 'antisaccharism', and which we would now call a boycott. It met with an unprecedented success, Clarkson optimistically estimating that 'at least 300,000 people had abandoned the use of sugar.' But although a highly popular gambit, favoured even by economists since East Indian sugar, grown without the use of slave labour, was considerably cheaper, this part of the campaign faltered, mainly because it was not agreed on unanimously throughout the Society (both Newton and Wilberforce were opposed), and also because of the unavailability of the alternative sugar.

Other innovations were wholeheartedly successful. The famous Wedgwood Seal met with such approval that the fashionable sets adopted it, and it was reproduced on bracelets, snuffboxes, and hairpins all over the country. William Cowper's *A Negro's Lament* was set to music, and listened to at society gatherings, and at less unfashionable meeting points. And since prior to reform, petitioning Parliament was the only positive way to get the member's attention, the Society was enormously successful in organising the presentation of these signed affidavits of public opinion. If public opinion had been sufficient, the slave trade would have been swept away by this wave of national enthusiasm.

But Parliament is at heart traditional, and has a traditionalists' mistrust of sudden change, and it still feared the international repercussions of abolition. But when the Bastille fell in 1789 it seemed to the abolitionists that here at last was the moment when France would agree to abolish as well, for surely no revolutionary government would acquiesce to a continuance of the 'horrid trade'. They were never again to commit themselves to such a wrong assumption, for rather than hastening the advent of the age of freedom, equality, and brotherhood, the French Revolution extinguished the cause of liberalism in England for forty years.

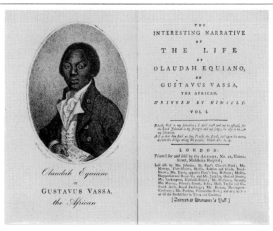

Equiano's auto-biography, published in 1789

Olaudah Equiano (opposite)

Charles James Fox

5. A Grateful Peasantry

'I ever have been and shall be a firm friend to our
present colonial system. I was bred in the good old
school, and taught to appreciate the value of our
West Indian possessions, and neither in the field nor
in the Senate shall their just rights be infringed whilst
I have an arm to fight in their defence or a tongue to
launch my voice against the damnable, cruel doctrine
of Wilberforce and his hypocritical allies; and I hope
my berth in heaven will be as exalted as his who would
certainly cause the murder of all our friends and
fellow-subjects in the colonies.'

(Lord Nelson, 1805)

When the fortunes of the abolitionists stood at their lowest ebb at the
turn of the century, this was typical of the opinion voiced against
them. Yet in 1789 victory must have seemed imminent, such was the
fervour of the feeling in the country. As the French Revolution began,
urging Charles Fox to declare: 'How much the greatest event it is that
ever happened in the world, and how much the best!' and as revolutionary fervour intoxicated England, the abolitionists must have
believed their moment had arrived. Thomas Clarkson· had been
dispatched post-haste to France to negotiate joint abolition. Thomas
Paine's book *The Rights of Man* had become obligatory reading for the
middle classes, who were standing by ready to seize any opportunity to
achieve fairer representation in the government of their affairs. The
establishment was cornered and outflanked. But the honeymoon was
shortlived. Clarkson discovered to his dismay that the French vested
interests were as solidly entrenched as their English counterparts, and
he was sent home from Paris in disgrace, accused of fomenting rebellion in the French Colony of San Domingo. The French Revolution
then lost the sense of its original purpose, indulging itself in a vengeful
and unnecessary orgy of blood letting, and the English, lovers of
moderation at all costs, took fright. The final blow was the French
declaration of war in 1793.

The flirtation with liberalism was over, and the shutters of conservatism were once more closed. The fearful populace took to looking for

Jacobins under their beds, and a reactionary wave now swept the island, prompting even the abolitionists to disassociate themselves from the dangerously republican and atheistic views of the revolutionaries. They had already lost a considerable amount of support in 1791 when the French Colony of San Domingo had been shaken by a violent and bloody slaves' revolt. The slaves had risen and massacred the white planters and their families, and tales of their atrocities had been eagerly disseminated through England by the anti-abolitionists, and this revolt was used as a terrifying example of what could be expected in the British Colonies if the meddlesome policies of emancipation were to be allowed to flourish. The Abolition Society went to great lengths to stress that their intention was to abolish the trade and ameliorate the conditions of the slaves, not emancipate them. But their voice was drowned beneath the widely broadcast prognostications of anarchy, confusion and murder. It was a bitter reversal of fortunes, which led to the acceptance of the Lord Chancellor Dundas' proposal for gradual abolition being accepted by an eager House of Commons, despite Fox's impassioned and eloquent plea against moderation. 'How can you carry on a trade in moderation?' he asked. 'How can a country be pillaged and destroyed in moderation? . . . We cannot modify injustice, the question is to what period we shall prolong it. Some think we should be unjust for ten years; others appear to think it is enough to be unjust for five years. Others that the present century should continue in disgrace, and that justice should commence its operation with the opening of another . . . there is an argument that has not been used at all, but it is the foundation of the whole business. I mean the difference of colour! Suppose a Bristol ship were to go to France, where the utmost fury of civil war is reported to prevail, and the democrats were to sell the aristocrats or vice versa, to be carried to Jamaica and sold as slaves, such a transaction would strike every man with horror, and why? Because they are of our colour! . . . My honourable friends, I believe this traffic to be impolitic; I know it be inhuman; I am certain it is unjust. It is so inhuman that if the plantations cannot be cultivated without it, they ought not to be cultivated at all . . . This table is never loaded with petitions, but where the people of England feel an actual grievance, and the House ought to feel itself bound to give a remedy.'

It was a famous debate and one in which Pitt was to give his wholehearted support to the abolition cause for the last time. Wilberforce had suggested to him that he speak on the civilising of Africa. 'Why first and last, ought the slave trade to be abolished? Because it is a noxious plant, under whose shade nothing that is useful or profitable

94

f der Französchen Colonie St: Domingo von d

From a report of the slave revolt in the French colony of San Domingo

to Africa will ever flourish or take root,' he told the House. 'We cannot wait for other nations to act with us. Ours is the largest share of the trade, ours the deepest guilt. We cannot wait until a thousand favourable circumstances unite together. Year after year escapes, and the evils go unredressed. We may wait, we may delay to cross the stream before us until it has run down, but we shall wait forever, for the river will still flow on unexhausted. Let no one say that Africa labours under a natural incapacity for civilisation, that providence has doomed her to be a nursery of slaves. Human sacrifice, my honourable friends, was once practised in these islands, and Britons have been sold as slaves to Rome! Might not some Roman Senator have pointed at the British Barbarians and said "*there* is a people never destined to be free". We were once as obscure among the nations of the earth, as savage in our manners, as debased in our morals, as degraded in our understandings, as these unhappy Africans are at present. If we listen to the voice of reason and duty, and pursue this day the line of conduct they prescribe . . .'

It is legendary that at this moment in his speech, the rising sun illuminated the eastern window of the chamber. '. . . some of us may live to see the reverse of that picture from which we now turn our eyes with shame and regret. We may behold the beams of science and philosophy breaking in upon their land, which at some happy period, in still later times, may blaze with full lustre, may illuminate and invigorate the most distant extremities of that immense continent. Then may we hope that even Africa, though last of all the quarters of the globe, shall enjoy at length, in the evening of her days, those blessings which were descended so plentifully upon us . . .'

But although he assured the House and Wilberforce in particular that he would vote against Dundas' proposed amendment, and that he would 'oppose to the utmost every proposition which in any way may tend either to prevent or even to postpone for an hour the total abolition of the slave trade', the House was not to be deterred from its purpose by fine oratory, and that purpose was the subtle negation of any proposed threat to its property. So they voted eagerly for the amendment carrying it by 230 votes to 85, knowing full well that gradual abolition in practical terms spelt 'never'. Likewise they even passed the motion suggesting 1796 as the year abolition should be initiated, knowing full well that nothing would be done when that date came round. They were proved right. For thanks to the undaunted conservatism of their attitude, the slave trade continued without mitigation, an attitude well expressed by Chancellor Dundas in the debate, when he suggested they should proceed with 'measures which should

96

not invade the property of individuals nor shock too suddenly the prejudices of our West Indian islands'.

It is perhaps difficult to understand how the cause for abolition could have proceeded so far and with such massive public support, and yet have failed repeatedly to make any great headway whenever it was debated in the Houses of Parliament. Yet the character of the Clapham Sect of Abolitionists itself supplies part of the answer to this problem. For the band of 'saints', although wholeheartedly opposed, with four notable exceptions, to the 'wickedness' of the slave trade, never chose to disassociate themselves from or even condemn those who grew so rich on the system they so despised. The planters saw themselves as kindly benefactors, subscribing heavily to the myth that they had rescued the African from darkness, and bestowed on him the fruits of a Christian civilisation, but the paradoxical point about this is that the abolitionists also subscribed to this absurd view. The men bent on reform were at great pains not to insult or condemn this rich and powerful class of people, preferring to attack the system and not the men who ran it. The planters helped them greatly in this, by glibly asserting they themselves were the tools of a trade they had not invented, and that they were devoting their energies towards the up-keep of a flourishing economy. The richer abolitionists such as Wilber-force, Buxton, and Brougham rubbed shoulders constantly with their opponents, as they shared mutual interests in most things except slavery, and even then they often had common ground in their religious beliefs. Naturally their respective interpretations of the scriptures vis-à-vis the enslavement of their fellow men differed widely, but the 'Saints'

William Wilberforce standing in the library of Henry Thornton's house in Battersea Rise. He lived there from 1804 to 1808 and it became the centre of the Clapham Sect. The sketch was made by one of the Thornton children

never attacked the established Church for dipping its hand in this particular till. For the Church as a body condoned slavery, and produced many Christian apologists to defend this contradictory view. The Reverend Raymond Harris, perhaps the best known of them all, was able to perform the most incredible metaphysical contortions, managing even to interpret that most unsuitable of Christian maxims 'Do unto others as you would have them do unto you' to the satisfaction of the pro-slavery element in the established Church. His argument was that the slave owner must treat his slave 'with the same tenderness, justice and humanity as he would have his slave behave to him were the slave the master and he himself the slave,' and equally every slave must serve his master 'with the same fidelity, submission and respect which he would expect from his master were the latter his slave and himself the master'. Not only was the established Church happy to accept these preposterous justifications, but naturally they also gave great satisfaction to the Christian merchants and plantation owners, who attended their churches on Sundays, having spent their week getting rich on the profits of slaving.

The Church, had it not been so heavily committed to the protection of private property and wealth, could have lent considerable weight to the abolition movement when it was most needed. But besides paying occasional lip service to the improvement of the lot of the slaves on the plantations, exhorting the planters to be just and compassionate towards their bondsmen and to instil in them the benefits of a Christian understanding of life, it never took any practical steps towards reformation or amelioration. It was left to the Dissenting Churches to try to improve the conditions of the slaves, but their missionaries had an impossible task since they were hated by the planters and by their managers, who suspected them of spreading sedition. Nothing in fact could have been further from their basic intention, for the dissenters also mistrusted revolution, instead preferring to educate the poor and enslaved into a proper acceptance of their lot. They were in no sense of the word radical, their zeal being directed purely towards conversion, baptism, and religious education. But to the planters this was potentially explosive, and believing in the maxim of a little learning being a dangerous thing, they feared any education would heighten the danger of revolt. So they persecuted the missionaries endlessly, and staunchly opposed any suggested amelioration of the condition of the slaves. In the West Indies the teachings of the Church were universally preferred.

The hypocrisy of the Church's attitude and the selfishness of the plantation owners should have been priority targets for the early abolitionists. But with the exception of Granville Sharp, none of them took time out to attack or refute their arguments. Sharp, in his *Just Limitation of Slavery in the Laws of God* and in his essay on self love, exploded with ease the tenuous justifications of apologists like the Reverend Raymond Harris, but none of the Clapham Sect directed any real ire against the planters. London society was still dazzled by the wealth and sophistication displayed by these returning millionaires, and the public by and large still naïvely believed in the planters philanthropy and munificence as projected best by certain plays on the London stage, such as *The Benevolent Planters* by Thomas Bellamy, and in the propaganda vehicles published by the Society of West Indian Planters and Merchants. The hand of this opposing society was greatly strengthened after the revolt in San Domingo and the reign of terror in France, for after these events, all it had to do was appeal to the Englishman's love of his property and inform him that an end to slavery meant revolution and an end to property. Their propaganda machine backed up this ever-ready threat with warnings of commercial benefits to France and even loss of the sugar colonies to America. It is therefore easy to understand why the abolition movement in the 1790s was so constantly stone-walled and why the Mother of Parliaments preferred to hide her eyes from England's national shame.

Worse was to follow. For the French Revolution at its bloodiest was followed by the catastrophic threat of invasion when France declared war on England. Even as Wilberforce prepared to battle for his cause in Parliament, Pitt was being distracted by these pressing foreign affairs, and Wilberforce was enjoined by Windham not to try 'to mend a house in a hurricane'. The abolition movement was about to run at its lowest ebb. Wilberforce and Pitt were falling out. Pitt had already been suspected of only espousing the cause of abolition for economic reasons, backed up by foreign policy, ever since it had been discovered that nearly all of the African slaves exported by Britain to foreign colonies went to San Domingo. When the slaves rose up there in 1791, a grave threat was posed to the retention of this valuable outlet, so two years later Pitt and Dundas sanctioned a military invasion of the island, which was successful and later led to the capture of Guadeloupe, Martinique, and St Lucia. So ironically enough during the years that Pitt was urging Wilberforce to speak out against the slave trade, Britain was actually doubling the amount of slaves she exported from Africa. And during the Napoleonic Wars, five more islands were added to the list. In 1794 the British were driven out of San Domingo, but undeterred, Pitt spent £3 million in the next two years in trying to recapture the island. Wilberforce remained silent during all this economic and political chicanery, although sternly rebuked by his close associate James Stephens, who failed to understand Wilberforce condoning the presence of troops in an island now run by slaves. His only remark during this controversy was one made opposing the ultimate withdrawal of the troops from the island.

It was clear the movement was floundering. It was unhappy within itself, and disillusioned with its mentor, William Pitt. Pitt, ever conscious of his priorities, gave his full attention to the protection of England, and turned his back on abolition. Wilberforce, bitterly disappointed, lost his impetus, and struggled to keep his political integrity. A man nominally dedicated to the liberty of his brother, he was now to be found supporting the Acts of Suppression. Worried that the French Revolution was spreading not only seditious political beliefs, but also encouraging atheism, he voted for them in the conviction that they were 'invigorating the constitution'. He was, at heart, a political conservative, so he could find nothing pricking his conscience when Habeas Corpus was suspended in 1794, and when in the following year all unlicensed public meetings were banned. He even refused to condemn the forcible emigration of slaves from Jamaica to the newly won and uncultivated Trinidad, in 1797.

It seemed that Wilberforce was slipping more and more into an apathetic frame of mind. Perhaps it was a natural reaction to the dashing of all his early hopes. He was shattered by the defection of Pitt and frightened of the dangers threatened from across the Channel, while at home he personally was subjected to ridicule and abuse. A frail man, and a sensitive one, he certainly collected a lot of hard blows over a short period of time, and now his thrust and energy deserted him, with the consequence that the movement nearly collapsed. It was ironic that it should happen at this time, for during this period of lost faith and inactivity, the motion for abolition came nearer than ever to being passed, failing by only four votes in 1796, and by the same margin in 1798. Had the impetus of the earlier years been maintained, and had Pitt not withdrawn his wholehearted support at such a crucial moment, the motion might well have been carried. As it was from 1797 to 1804 the Society for Abolition did not meet at all, and in those years the only amendment made to the slave trade was an Act passed widening the space between the decks on the Guineamen, and regulating the number of slaves allowed to be carried on board. Chancellor Dundas's proposed 'gradualism' was proving all too successful.

Wilberforce was now almost without allies. His old-time supporter Burke died in 1797, having spent his last few years obsessed by a loathing for Jacobinism. The rift with his close friend Pitt was deepening, Windham, once an abolitionist, had now changed sides, and finally

William Pitt, the Younger, by J. Hoppner

Fox and his closest associates deserted the House for nearly five years in a somewhat useless demonstration of their displeasure at Parliament's indifference. The public's attention had turned to the war, and Dundas used the threat from Napoleon as an excuse to countenance no further discussion concerning abolition during the hostilities. Pitt became increasingly involved in the war, an involvement that was to sever entirely his partnership with Wilberforce and finally to end his own life. With England distracted and the colonies hostile to any interference with their livelihood, the task of actually achieving abolition must have seemed ever more Herculean.

The sugar-producing colonies were well aware of the proposals being made by the abolitionists, and protested vociferously whenever Parliament attempted to interfere in their domestic affairs. They had already been advised to improve the conditions of slavery in the islands, and while not openly hostile to amelioration, they made little attempt to put any such proposal into practice. Life for the planters had settled into a very agreeable pattern, so they strongly resented any attempt to regulate or alter their profitable and luxurious existence. Lady Nugent, the wife of the Governor of Jamaica, wrote in her *Journals* of the indolent and extravagant society enjoyed by the West Indian whites. Although in sympathy with the abolition movement, and a lady of compassion and good humour, she was so divorced from the realities of plantation life that she was moved to write that 'generally speaking I believe the slaves are extremely well used'.

Undoubtedly there were well-cared-for slaves, and well-ordered plantations, as there were benevolent planters. Samuel Martin who lived in Antigua did not buy a slave for twenty years because his own had increased so plentifully under his beneficent guardianship, but he was probably the exception rather than the rule. It would also be as unfair to assume that all planters were as murderous as Arthur Hodge of Tortula who was executed for murdering sixty of his slaves, or Edward Huggins of Nevis who escaped punishment for publicly flogging thirty of his slaves 'to the tune of 240 lashes each'. The truth lay somewhere between these two extremes, but as the plantations grew richer, and absenteeism became more rife among the owners, there were certainly more men like Huggins in charge rather than men like Martin. Because the schools were so desperately inadequate in the West Indies, planters naturally sent their children back to school in England, and since very few young men ever returned to the monotonous and sometimes dangerous life in the Caribbean, managers were employed to run their estates for them, and having no vested interest in the preservation of the property of which they were in charge, they

Lady Maria Nugent by John Downman

were much less inclined to exercise a humane jurisdiction over the slaves. They were also paid inadequate wages, on average between £150 and £200 a year, so they usually enriched themselves at the absent owners' expense in order to buy plantations of their own. Maria Nugent observed at the time that 'these people eat like cormorants and drink like porpoises' and besides their barbarous social behaviour, it was standard practice for them to keep a succession of black mistresses. Illegitimacy was the rule rather than the exception. But because of this interbreeding a brown middle class was being created, the existence of which in the West Indies helped to prevent the extreme polarisation of the races which took place in the United States.

It was an immoral and corrupt society. It affected the style of Imperial behaviour, but all it could actually boast was an endless round of drunken balls, and gluttonous dinner parties, fronted by extravagant displays of wealth and riddled by obsessive gambling. As the plantations expanded and more slaves were imported, the massive increase in the number of blacks on the islands led the planters to panic. The fear of what had happened in Haiti, and the possibility of similar revolutions in the British islands was the constant topic of conversation. Laws were passed requiring the employment of a number of whites on each plantation, which served the dual purpose of keeping black slaves out of skilled jobs, and providing the estates with armed defenders. The penal code was made even more stringent, and the slightest misdemeanour was punished even more viciously. Lady Nugent, in her *Journal*, mentions seeing the heads of executed slaves impaled on spikes, but is not moved to make a disapproving comment. A religious woman, and an admirer of Wilberforce, Lady Nugent gradually accepted the notion of abolition, while most of her contemporaries in the Caribbean either accepted the lot of the blacks without question, or were violently opposed to any interference with their own brutal, lazy and immoral way of life. Lady Nugent despaired of ever being able to persuade the negroes to improve their own moral standards while their white masters set such a low example. West Indian promiscuity and illegitimacy was to be an obsession with governors' wives for the next 150 years, but how many of them realised that it was never an African pattern but a pattern imposed by slavery?

With the fortunes of his cause at their lowest ebb, William Wilberforce was silent in Parliament, from 1800 to 1803 not even attempting to move his resolution, and at home he spent his time in prayer and contemplation. Clarkson had retired, the Committee lay disbanded. It seemed as if the West Indian interest at last had got the upper hand.

By 1806 the tide was turning once more in the Society's favour. Anti-Jacobinism was dead, thanks to Napoleon, and the public had not forgotten the cause. The work of the new philanthropists such as Jeremy Bentham, founder of Utilitarianism, and Dr Porteous, the Evangelical Archbishop of Canterbury, were widely read. Strangest of all, even some of the Caribbean planters were considering an experimental abolition, unfortunately not inspired by any sudden conversion to Humanism, but motivated by their usual self-interest. Britain had newly acquired certain Dutch and French territories in the West Indies, including Trinidad and Guyana, which were highly fertile but as yet uncultivated for sugar. So certain West Indians, fearing the possibility of new and dangerous competition, proposed stopping the slave trade for a number of years so that their rivals would be deprived of labour. Certainly the confidence of the West Indian interests was clearly shaken, particularly by the dramatic fall of their sugar imports into England after a massive increase in the cost of the commodity. Furthermore, the Industrial Revolution in England was giving the country a dramatic face lift, in which the continuation of the slave trade would appear as even more of a ridiculous anachronism. So

Johnny enjoying the sports of the field.

A cartoon lampooning life on the West Indian plantations

Spanish Town, Jamaica, from an engraving of 1774. King's House, which can be seen on the right of the picture, is shown in the photograph below left

A View of the King's House and Public Offices at S.t Jago de la Vega.
Published as the Act directs July 1.t 1774.

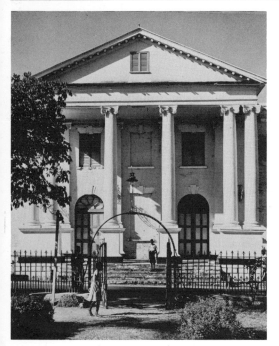

Rose Hall (right), a plantation 'great house' near Montego Bay. The photograph on the facing page shows the building before restoration

Speightstown, Barbados — sometimes called 'Little Bristol', which remains much as it was in the early nineteenth century

finally, in 1804, the Committee for the Abolition of the Slave Trade convened once more, after a silence of seven years.

There were new members now, the most distinguished being Lord Brougham, James Stephen and Zachary Macaulay. Fox had returned to the House of Commons, and the Act of Union had imported a new and influential membership, the Irish, who as disinterested parties in this controversy were willing and ready to lend the abolitionists their support. So in the May of that year Wilberforce once again moved his resolution to bring in a Bill, and once again found Pitt, still Prime Minister, at his side. This time Wilberforce was successful, and the Bill passed three readings in the House of Commons, but was baulked by the Lords, who put off a division on the Bill until the following session, knowing full well that this meant a return to square one for the abolitionists.

However, they refused to be shaken and in the February of the following year Wilberforce once more introduced his Bill. But now he suffered his bitterest disappointment, for the moment he most needed Prime Ministerial support was the moment Pitt chose to desert him. Tired by the Napoleonic wars, thwarted by the King's hostility to Fox from forming the National coalition he so desired, and in bad health, Pitt refused to spend any more energy on a subject he now considered to be a side issue. He even tried to stall Wilberforce, but Wilberforce was not to be cheated at this late date, and bravely pushed ahead. But the House was more hostile this session, having been worked by the West Indians into another state of panic about emancipation and its possible consequences. Wilberforce went to great lengths to assure the House that the Society for Abolition in no way advocated the manumission of the negroes until they were fit and ready for it, but to no avail. And with the surprise defection of the Irish members, the Bill was defeated on its second reading by seven votes.

Another propaganda war then followed, with the indefatigable Clarkson being dragged out of retirement in order to tour the country and test public opinion. But certainly no further progress in Parliament would have been made had not the Prime Minister died in 1806. Many abolitionists had always accused Pitt of only paying lip service to their cause while actually refusing to support it at the crucial moments, and even Wilberforce accused him of governing by influence rather than by principle. But that in itself is a naïve assessment of the ritual of government, and an unfair epitaph for his once closest friend. For although Pitt did indeed desert him at the vital moment, he had always up until then given Wilberforce his unswerving support in Parliament, and had only once failed to put this support into words.

Whether his desire to achieve abolition was genuine or not, or whether he was fired purely by economic rather than philanthropic motives, it is impossible to say. But it is quite certain that without the Prime Minister's support in the House, Wilberforce would have found it considerably more difficult if not actually impossible to command any formal attention for his radical proposal. Particularly when it is remembered that not only were most of his parliamentary colleagues hostile to it, but also the King and the Royal Family. Pitt's adoption of the cause lent it the necessary authority.

But now William Pitt was dead, and in the eyes of many abolitionists discredited, the movement needed a new friend in the government. They found him in Charles James Fox, now Foreign Secretary under Lord Grenville. Fox, the great liberal, the 'man of the people', had supported the abolitionist cause for many years, yet Wilberforce's great admiration of Pitt had blinded him to Fox's virtues. Wilberforce was too much the puritan, too Christian, to appreciate Fox, whose reputation as a drunkard, a compulsive gambler and womaniser had constantly been used to discredit his ability and his genuine passion for liberty.

With Pitt dead and Fox at last in power, it must have seemed strange to Wilberforce to ally himself with a man of whom in all else but his love of liberty he disapproved, and it must have afforded Fox, the old sinner, some genuine amusement to clap hands with the man who was called a saint.

The bargain was struck, and the abolition of the slave trade became what it had never been under Pitt and the Tories, it became at last, a government measure. 'If,' Fox told the House of Commons on 10 June 1806 as he rose to propose the enactment of abolition, 'during the almost forty years that I have now had the honour of a seat in Parliament, I had been so fortunate as to accomplish that and that only, I should think I had done enough, and could retire from public life with comfort and the conscious satisfaction that I had done my duty.'

The motion was carried by 114 to fifteen, and in the Lords by forty-one to thirty. Furthermore a slave Importation Restriction Bill was passed which restricted the transportation of slaves into any foreign colonies, forbade the export of slaves from one British Colony to another without licence, and prohibited foreign slave ships from using British ports.

From then on wholesale abolition was only a matter of time. New ships were prevented from entering the slave trade, and in the next session of Parliament, Lord Grenville's Government – having been returned at the General Election – immediately introduced the Aboli-

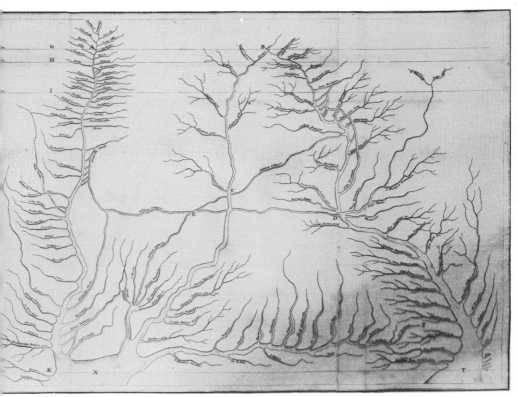

The efforts of the British and American abolitionists to cut down the tree of slavery —
from an Anti-slavery Society pamphlet

This 'map' from Thomas Clarkson's *History of the Abolition of the African Slave Trade*
(1808) shows the sources of the abolition movement as the tributaries of a great river

tion Bill into the House of Lords. It was carried there on its second reading by a hundred votes to thirty-six despite the vigorous opposition of the Duke of Clarence, who had opposed its course all the way along the line, Lord Hawkesbury and other 'West Indian' reactionaries, and in the same month was given its second reading in the House of Commons. Those who had fought for twenty years for this moment held their breath. Wilberforce himself said very little during these final debates, and his most voluble opponents, Castlereagh and Windham, were completely silent. It was left to the Solicitor General, Romilly, to make the final plea. 'When I look to the man at the head of the French Monarchy,' he told the packed House, 'distributing kingdoms to his family and principalities to his followers, seeming when he sits upon his throne to have reached the summit of human ambition, and the pinnacle of earthly happiness. When I follow that man to his closet or his bed, and consider the pangs with which his solitude must be tortured by the recollection of the blood he has spilled, and the oppressions he has committed – when I compare with those pangs of remorse the feelings which must accompany my honourable friend [Wilberforce] from this house to his home, after the vote of this night shall have confirmed the object of his unceasing labours, when he retires into the bosom of his happy and delighted family, when he lays himself down upon his bed, reflecting on the innumerable voices that will be raised in every quarter of the globe to bless him, how much more pure and perfect felicity must he enjoy in the consciousness of having preserved so many millions of his fellow creatures.'

The House rose to its feet and gave a standing ovation to the man whose greatest ambition was about to be realised while Wilberforce himself sat silently, in tears. The House voted overwhelmingly in favour of the Bill by 283 votes to sixteen, and on 25 March, 1807, it received the assent of the King. Wilberforce celebrated this famous victory with his friends in Clapham, and England indulged itself in an orgy of back-patting, as the country rejoiced at the victory 'in the greatest battle ever fought by human beings.' Schools were given a week's holiday, poems were composed in honour of the heroes, and Macaulay later wrote of it as 'one of the noblest designs which the world ever witnessed, delivering half the world from bondage and blood, and pouring upon it light, liberty, and civilisation.'

The Bill for Abolition stipulated that as from 1 January 1807 'all manner of dealing and trading in the purchase or transfer of slaves, or of persons intending to be sold in, at, or from any part of the coast or countries of Africa' was to be 'utterly abolished, prohibited, and declared to be unlawful.' Any ship under British colours which disobeyed was to be forfeited to the crown, and fines of £100 were to be levied for every slave illegally transported. A system of bounty rewards to the captors of slaves and slave ships was introduced, insurance contracts negotiated on behalf of the trade were to be penalised, and all slaves captured from the illegal slave ships were automatically to be forfeited to the Crown. Not knowing where they came from, the agents of the Crown merely dumped them in the new colony of Sierra Leone.

It was all very well intentioned but hopelessly inadequate, for although the British navy vigilantly policed the seas in search of lawbreakers, the rewards of a successful slave run were still so great that merchants and captains were prepared to take the risk of heavy fines, and there were African traders still ready and willing to supply them. Captain Crow, who made the last legal voyage of a British slaver, reported the dismay of his African friends at the news of abolition, and their amazement that the English King should want to take away their livelihoods.

An amendment was subsequently passed in 1811 which made trading punishable with transportation to Botany Bay, or to Van Diemen's Land, but again this terrifying prospect acted as only a minor deterrent, as can be judged from the figures. In the thirty years before abolition 120,000 slaves, conservatively estimated, survived the crossings each year to be offered for sale in the Americas. By 1835 this figure had risen to 150,000 a year, similarly conservatively estimated. In the seventy years after abolition, taken as a whole, the average annual decrease was one tenth of one per cent.

Other nations moved in to fill the gap, and the British carried on, using flags of convenience, of which the Stars and Stripes was favourite, for the United States, conscious of its new national dignity, refused to allow the British navy the right of search. There was an increased demand to be satisfied from the cotton plantations of the American South, and a growing trade to Brazil and other countries of South America. In short, in the years immediately after abolition the number of slaves exported from Africa actually increased. Until Parliament abolished slavery itself in 1834 and America followed a generation later, Wilberforce's immortal victory accomplished very little.

Wilberforce himself was in no great hurry to see actual emancipation enacted, and this was the main reason for the split that occurred within the abolition movement. The young radicals in the group saw the folly of being satisfied with just the abolition of the trade, and further argued that the Abolition Act was unenforceable. They wanted

113

slavery to be abolished simultaneously, and in the same session of Parliament that had seen that Abolition Bill enacted, a young radical named Earl Percy proposed a motion to introduce a Bill for the gradual abolition of slavery in the West Indian Colonies. But the House was practically deserted, and Percy found his only verbal opponent to be Wilberforce himself. For 'St Wilforce' – as he was known to his distant slave friends – once more disassociated himself from any notion of emancipation until the slaves were properly prepared for it, declaring himself and his colleagues as 'satisfied with having gained an object which is safely attainable'.

It was this refusal of the Claphamites to involve themselves immediately in the vital business of total emancipation which condemned the slave to another thirty years of penal captivity.

Leaving Sunderland harbour

Anchored, awaiting cargo

Shipping cargo at daybreak

Chased by English frigate *Active*

Cut out by the frigate's boats

Destruction of the slaver

Six paintings illustrating the history of the slave trader *Orange Grove*

6. Free Paper Come

'Men who can bear slavery most assuredly
offer a very strong presumption that they can
bear freedom.'

(Daniel O'Connell)

The Claphamites sense of satisfaction once they had reached their
'safely attainable' objective unfortunately only served as a brake on
the movement towards total emancipation. The other and greater
obstacle was the intransigent attitude of the colonists and planters
towards any proposed change in the structure of life on the West
Indian islands. They were suspicious of change, not because life in the
Caribbean was amenable, but because when the crop was good and
the harvest successful, the consequences were extremely rewarding for
all white men involved. Thus they developed a paranoic possessiveness
about their 'property', which for them included their slave labour
force, and became highly indignant whenever liberal opinion back in
England made plain both its disapproval of and its intention to reform
the planters' *modus vivendi*.

It was this bloodyminded stubborness that on the one hand made
the Act of Abolition a dead letter in the colonies and on the other hand
actually hastened their downfall. No doubt if the planters had made
any real attempt to carry out Canning's scheme of 'amelioration' and
had tolerated Parliament's half-hearted attempt to regulate their
domestic affairs, slavery would have continued to exist quite legally for
a considerably longer period. For the British Government was merely
proposing that the planters should try and improve the lot of their
slaves in their day-to-day existence, avoid unnecessarily severe or cruel
punishments, and gradually – over an unspecified number of years,
introduce full but supervised freedom. The Claphamite sect itself
would have been well satisfied if these proposals had been received
favourably, because they still clung to the naïve belief that since the
trade itself had been abolished, slavery would die a natural death. So
in the interim, as long as conditions were made more tolerable for the
slaves and provided they were educated into a Christian acceptance
of their future role, the senior abolitionists could retire from the fray
with untroubled consciences.

But the planters were unable to view the situation with any degree of

117

o slaves in Jamaica
ving tribal markings and
re devices for punishing
misdemeanours.

detachment, due mainly to their unbridled hatred of all abolitionists, neither were they able to gauge the actual strength of the public opinion arraigned against them in their homeland. They foolishly assumed such opposition as there was to spring from a handful of cranks, and this could be safely ignored since many of these 'cranks' were friendly with the absentee owners themselves. So they paid scant attention to any advice about improving the lot of their slaves, and remonstrated hysterically whenever the home government made any attempt to enforce orders-in-council from distant Downing Street. Thus after the Act of Abolition of 1807 life on the plantations remained virtually unchanged for another twenty years.

So once again the anti-slavery movement foundered. The senior members were tired, and the younger radical ones were powerless. England was suffering from post-war fatigue, and during the next few years prior to Reform the country became increasingly concerned with its own internal problems. Much energy and emotion had been spent on the campaign which had culminated in the Act of 1807, so the public could not altogether be blamed for the apathy it displayed whenever any attempt was made to rekindle its interest in the subject of slavery. Like Wilberforce and the senior abolitionists, it believed in the inevitable death of slavery once its life-line had been severed, and besides, the West Indies were a long way away. While the trade itself had flourished from the major ports in England, it had been easier to draw people's attention to the national disgrace. It now required a completely new campaign to be mounted in order to fire public interest in the fate of the slaves in the far distant Caribbean.

The purpose of the Abolition Act had been to curtail and outlaw the trade from Africa. But during this period of domestic indifference and colonial intransigence, it became increasingly apparent that thousands of slaves were still being smuggled into the West Indies, despite the energetic attempts of the Navy to police the seas. So in 1815 Wilberforce introduced a bill which had originally been designed by James Stephen, proposing a compulsory registration of all existing slaves in the colonies in an attempt to forestall further illegal importation. This had worked successfully in Trinidad a few years earlier, and later in St Lucia, but these were crown colonies without their own legislative assemblies. The colonies with their own legislative bodies such as Jamaica and Barbados protested bitterly, claiming such interference to be a gross violation of their rights and liberties. Castlereagh weakly attended to their remonstrations and withdrew the proposition, assuring the Commons that the colonies would set up their own registers voluntarily.

For once the rebellious colonies concurred, but it was a purely academic exercise, for all the islands except Tobago and Grenada failed to penalise the sale of unregistered slaves, and furthermore made little or no attempt to enforce registration. In 1819 Parliament was therefore obliged to enact that copies of these registers must be kept in London in an attempt to supervise illegal sales, and while this was a moderately successful action, it also had an unforeseen and unfortunate consequence. For surely a piece of legislation such as The Registry Act, as the more radical abolitionists argued at the time, only helped to ratify the hotly disputed point about the right of one man to hold legal ownership over another? So, ironically, what started out as a humanely intended piece of legislation ended up as a precedent the planters themselves used in the ensuing battle for compensation.

The planters' other great fear, besides that of loss of property, was insurrection. There was always a danger of this on the plantations, since riots and disturbances were common, but when the slaves organised themselves well enough to mount a revolt they were easily defeated, and the planters used these incidents as propaganda, and by the skilful broadcasting of inflated tales of negro atrocities, they built up a potent case for non-interference in their domestic affairs. Nowadays we still hear echoes of these arguments as the black fights for equality. In those days he was fighting for his freedom.

Already in the islands there were fresh rumours circulating amongst the slaves themselves. Planters often discussed inflammatory subjects such as emancipation in front of their servants in the arrogant belief that they could neither hear the conversations nor understand their implications. And since the talk at this time was all about Wilberforce, the proposals for total emancipation and the effects of the Abolition Act, it was only to be expected that new stories would start circulating and in their circulation would become wildly exaggerated. The strongest and most widely believed rumour was that freedom had already been granted to the slaves by Parliament and that the planters were withholding it from them. It spread from plantation to plantation that 'free paper come', and from island to island. Barbados was the first to mutiny. The slaves rose up, burnt and destroyed a considerable amount of property, but contrary to the expectation of a general massacre no whites were killed. Needless to say, hundreds of slaves died and many more were summarily executed, but these facts were hardly good weapons in the planters' propaganda warfare. So they simply played on the revolt itself, pointing out that this was the inevitable result of interference from abroad, of indulgent liberalism, of interfering missionaries and a misguided mother parliament. Leave us

119

THE

ANTI-SLAVERY RECORD.

VOL. I. OCTOBER, 1835. [SECOND EDITION.] NO. 10.

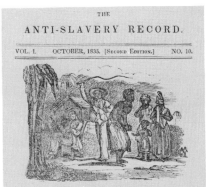

THE FLOGGING OF FEMALES.

"What!—the whip on WOMAN's shrinking flesh?"

Some of our readers may think the flogging of females a very rare and extraordinary occurrence. It is nevertheless very common. The cut above is no exaggerated representation of an everyday scene in the past history of the West Indies. In 1824, Great Britain endeavored to ameliorate Slavery in its colonies, and among other things to abolish the flogging of females. After a series of shameful evasions, the legislature of Jamaica, in Dec. 1827, held the following language. "The whip is not forbidden in the field, lest the abandonment, too suddenly, of a long-established usage, should be misunderstood by the slaves. * * * Until negro women have acquired more of the sense of shame, which distinguishes European females, it will be impossible with respect to them, to lay aside altogether punishment by flogging, there being no substitute that promises to be accompanied with the same salutary dread." That similar scenes are witnessed daily in these United States, though perhaps not in mercy's sight, take the testimony of Rev. David Nelson, a man who has been a Slaveholder, and has spent his whole life among Slaveholders, and whose veracity few will dare to impeach. He says to Christian slaveholders, "You help to put it out of the power

Ladies Whipping Girls.   Page 109.

THE

ANTI-SLAVERY RECORD.

VOL. I.   MAY, 1835.   NO. 5.

CRUELTIES OF SLAVERY.

When we narrate the cruelties of individual masters upon their slaves, it is not for the purpose of exciting public indignation against those masters, nor of drawing the inference, that all masters are equally cruel; but to show that cruelty is the fruit of the system. Every tree must be known by its fruits. Cruelty may occur under good and impartial laws, but then it is in spite of the laws, not in consequence of them. On the other hand, where the laws themselves violate rights, make one class the property of another, and withhold redress of wrongs, cruelty, in ten thousand forms, is the necessary result. If the amount of cruelty perpetrated upon the slaves of this republic could be known to the world,

Vol. I.   5

A Slave Plantation.   Page 94.

Illustrations from the *Anti-slavery Record*

A'NEGRO FESTIVAL drawn from Nature in the ISLAND of S.^T VINCENT.

A plantation-owner's version of the life of slaves in the West Indies

alone, they demanded, we know our own business best.

And alone they would have been left if it had been up to Canning and Castlereagh. But other forces were at work, most significantly a dramatic weakening in the position of the sugar colonies themselves. They had always been economically unstable, subject to either sudden disaster or to runaway success, but now their economic importance was being stringently reassessed due to the growing belief in free trade. The monopoly that had for so long protected the West Indian sugar commerce was thought by some to be unhealthy and uneconomic, the price of slave-grown sugar now being actually higher than the 'free' sugar cultivated in the East Indies. A growing body of critics were actually recommending getting rid of the Caribbean colonies altogether. The planters must have been aware of this, since from the 1790s onwards the petitions to Parliament from the West Indies became more and more concerned with the abolition of sugar dues and less and less to do with arguing the need for slavery. The petitions finally became obsessed with compensation when the West Indies understood the inevitability of their fate.

The other force at work was a revival within the abolition movement itself. Wilberforce, now in a much weakened state of health, and aware that he had failed in not pressing much earlier for 'clean' emancipation, stepped down from the leadership and Thomas Buxton was persuaded to take his place. There could not have been a more dramatic contrast between the new leader and the old, Buxton being an ox-like man, slow of thought and dull in speech, compared with Wilberforce's diminutive stature and quicksilver rhetoric. But they shared a mutual obsession in abolition, and in the Christian righteousness of their campaign. Buxton may have been a laughable figure to some of his younger contemporaries, but his dedication to the task was phenomenal.

In 1823 the London Society for the Mitigation and Gradual Abolition of Slavery was founded and immediately the petitions recommending abolition started to flood Parliament once more, 750 being presented in the first year and a half alone. The society was much stronger than before and was now presided over by the Duke of Gloucester, giving it an added aura of respectability. The pamphlet war was restarted, which included the publication of Wilberforce's tract laboriously titled *An Appeal to Religion, Justice and Humanity of the Inhabitants of the British Empire in Behalf of the Negro Slaves in the West Indies*. The *Anti-Slavery Monthly Reporter* now first appeared as well, and in 1825 Macaulay took over as editor of this most influential journal. The movement was back to where it was between 1785 and

1792 with its successful saturation of the country with propaganda, but now it was far more muscular and even more energetic. By 1832 there were 1200 affiliated societies throughout the country, a much younger and more radical membership, and in the days immediately prior to the first reformed Parliament, a much wider audience. For in 1832 the vote was extended to the occupants of houses with a rateable value of over £10, which meant that many of the working class were admitted to the franchise for the first time, and most of these new votes were predictably enough opposed to the notion of slavery. Women were being admitted to the meetings now as well, and were doing remarkable work within the Society itself, not without first having to overcome considerable opposition from the male element. But while all these exciting changes were taking shape within the movement, another series of setbacks had first to be suffered in the shape of further violent disturbances in the colonies.

Canning was determined to press for the completion of his 'amelioration' policy, and this seemed to suit the mood of the new Parliament when it convened in 1823. After all, it was an enormous step, they argued, to disturb the social and economic life of the West Indies, so surely it was wiser to give the colonists one last chance to set their own house in order? This hesitant and uncourageous attitude sentenced the slaves in the Caribbean to another ten years of bondage, while the mother of Parliaments sat on her hands, waiting benignly for the impossible to occur. Canning's speech of intention was relayed to the West Indies, as were the expressions of his earnest desire to see his suggested reforms carried out at once, a list of proposals which included the prohibition of the whip for driving gangs and punishing women slaves. This itself was a grave tactical mistake, for the whip was held to be 'The Grand Badge of Slavery' and was therefore synonomous with the state of servitude. Do away with the whip, and according to the slaves themselves, you do away with slavery. Thus rumours of its proposed prohibition confirmed the slaves' belief in impending emancipation, with the result that the planters became even more paranoically nervous and in Jamaica actually hanged eleven slaves on mere suspicion.

Dissatisfaction spread everywhere, and in Barbados the 'poor' whites were encouraged to attack the white missionary William Shrewsbury, who was accused of spreading inflammatory information and ideas. They broke up his chapel, attacked his congregation and forced him off the island. In Demerara 13,000 slaves then revolted, but this time they spilt blood. They killed two overseers on one estate and in the subsequent fighting one other soldier was wounded. Over one hundred slaves lost their lives. And again, once the revolt was quelled, vengeance on the blacks was frightful. Over forty more slaves were hanged and an unknown number flogged, tortured, or imprisoned. The white missionary John Smith, who had been largely responsible for the restraint shown by the rebels, was tried and sentenced to death, and although a recommendation for mercy was made due to his failing health, he died in prison before the pardon reached him.

These events in the colonies had directly conflicting results. It seemed on the one hand that once more the abolitionist cause was going to suffer as it had earlier under the anti-Jacobin backlash which followed the French Revolution. Certainly Parliament was frightened by the noisy remonstrations made by the West Indian cause, frightened enough to cling vainly to the notion of amelioration in preference to any more direct policy of emancipation. It was also frightened enough not to try and enforce it. All the 'free' as opposed to crown colonies refused point blank to entertain Canning's latest set of lukewarm palliatives, again threatening to switch their allegiance away from the crown to the United States of America, even though it was highly unlikely that America would have enjoyed having to bolster up such an ailing economy. But the British Government still remained idle, accepting Canning's assertion that the colonies would voluntarily mend their ways. On the other hand this setback only strengthened the abolitionist cause, because even the moderates began to sense that the amelioration policy was proving to be a non-starter. Secondly, there was an amazing outcry over the attack on William Shrewsbury and the death of John Smith. While thousands of black slaves were still being flogged to work, starved of food, whipped for insubordination, castrated, mutilated or hanged for other felonies, and turned out on the streets when too old to be of further use, Parliament was quite content to support a policy of gradual abolition. But as soon as one white missionary had his chapel demolished and was forcibly exiled and another died of consumption in gaol it was scandalised. In 1824 and 1825 the House sat transfixed while the stories of the missionaries and their terrible fates were related in detail. And even though Canning actually managed to prevent a motion of censure being passed on the colonies, the spark had at last found its way to the bonfire.

In 1826 Parliament was presented with a petition for abolition of slavery signed by seventy-two thousand people, and Canning himself felt the need to try once more to enforce his will on the contumacious colonies. But once more they resisted him, still mouthing assurances that they would ameliorate conditions if left to themselves. Little did the planters realise that they were thus busily shaping the noose with which they were about to hang themselves, for the British public's patience was wearing paper thin. 'The progress of the colonies is so slow,' declared one member of Parliament, 'as to be imperceptible to all human eyes save their own.' The Abolition Society noted the growing impatience in England, and when the great meeting took place in the Freemason's Hall in 1830, over 2000 attended. The movement was now split down the middle over policy, the young radicals demanding instant abolition, while the old guard still advised caution. Wilberforce took the chair, but his voice was drowned by the exuberance and determination of the younger and more forceful members. A subcommittee was formed, calling itself the Agency Committee, and this body was responsible for the revival of the system of national propaganda tours. This time, however, the agents, mostly unpaid volunteers, were instructed to spend their time in persuading their audiences of the illegality of slavery and not to dwell on tales of atrocities and injustice. This formidable new machinery was once more inspired by the energy and financed by the money of the Quakers, that most philanthropic and open-handed body of people, without whose support the abolition movement might well have collapsed. And this new wave of enthusiasm even inspired a government more obsessed with the crisis of Reform and domestic disorder, to have one last go at the colonies. Another order-in-council, far more severe than any of its precedents, was imposed on the crown colonies and the others were instructed to follow suit. This order met with even more stubborn resistance, and once more the resultant dissatisfaction voiced by the planters transmuted itself to the slaves, with the consequence that the colonies were faced with their most dangerous insurrection to date, that of Jamaica in December, 1831.

The Jamaican uprising was the last and the biggest rebellion prior to emancipation, and repeated only on a larger scale the pattern of the earlier revolts in Demerara and Barbados. Day-to-day existence on the plantations had not altered drastically since the Act of Abolition, although a number of slaves now held slightly more exalted positions in the household or in the field, and a complicated pattern of relationships between the planters and their headmen had grown up, based on mutual loyalty and in many cases on actual blood relationships. There was considerably more change in the towns, for the ports of Jamaica had become very active trading centres, and the merchant class were now as important in the life of the island as the old plantocracy. The use of slaves in the more complex business of an urban trading economy produced a semi-educated group quite unlike the field slave of a century earlier. Moreover, there was now a sizeable class of free

125

coloured inhabitants, some even with slaves of their own, and a much larger number of poor whites and halfcastes.

Perhaps the most significant change in Jamaica had been the intense success of the Baptist mission, and all over the island churches had sprung up following the foundation of the first chapel by George Lisle, an emancipated slave who had landed in Jamaica after the War of American Independence. The Baptist Society in England was later prevailed upon to send out missionaries, who successfully survived the constant persecution meted out to them by the planters, who suspected them of spreading subversive doctrines. It is one of the most notable paradoxes of the whole paradoxical history of Abolition that while Wilberforce and the Clapham Sect believed in emancipation only through Christian conversion, the planters' biggest fear was the subversion of their slaves' minds by Christianity.

The Baptist Church nonetheless established a great hold over the negro, and if the planters had been a little less shortsighted they would have realised that as such the orthodox Baptist Church posed no threat at all to their security, for in essence it was conservative and peaceable, desiring only to convert the slave to Christian ways and dedicated to the gradual improvement of his daily round. The real threat lay in the Bush or Native Baptist sect, who interpreted the Bible as a manifesto of revolution or dispensed with it altogether and preached salvation through dreams. The congregation was encouraged to dream, and the 'Daddies' or ministers would interpret these, in the search for some divine significance. If this was discovered, the individual was then directed to baptism. This underground church was the church of the potential rebel, for its ministers were usually exiles from the orthodox Baptist movement. One such minister was Daddy Sharp, a household slave in the service of a merchant in Montego Bay. A mysterious figure, Sharp played all the roles, loyal servant, deacon of the orthodox Baptist Church, minister of his own Bush Baptists and revolutionary. He was called 'the director of the whole', the man held responsible for organising the Jamaica uprising.

Although Sharp was undoubtedly the main force behind the rebellion, his plan was basically a completely peaceful one, more resembling a programme of civil disobedience rather than bloodthirsty mayhem. He had heard all the rumours in circulation about emancipation, and whether he himself believed them or not he was determined to make them come true. Certainly many of his followers believed that the King had made them free, and that not only were the whites illegally withholding their freedom from them, but were 'making a studiation' to kill all the black men and keep only the black women. Sharp knew that many of the Bush Baptists were in favour of a more blood-thirsty rebellion than he had in mind, so he pressed for moderation, urging his followers merely to go on strike after Christmas and not to return to work until freedom was granted. It was not a very carefully organised campaign at all. Instead it was more a general directive to the slaves to mount a peaceful demonstration in the hope that their masters would be sufficiently intimidated to grant them the freedom which they believed was now their legal right.

On the island at this time was another man who held great influence over the negroes, the white missionary William Knibb who had arrived in Jamaica in 1825. He was a man of great passion and zeal and of more than controversial character, but committed to saving the souls of the slaves by orthodox Baptism and not by fomenting rebellion. Nevertheless, like other missionaries, he was loathed and feared by the white planters, who persecuted him remorselessly. He too heard the rumours about emancipation and about the uprising from members of his congregation, and was plagued with the endlessly asked question: 'Has free paper come?' Terrified of the consequences if he gave them any assurances on this matter, he hotly denied it and threatened expulsion on any member of his Church who persisted in spreading the lie. Besides the fact that he knew emancipation had not been granted, he was also aware of how badly organised and ill equipped the slaves were for any intended insurrection.

But by now open rebellion was inevitable. Daddy Sharp was preaching with great eloquence and passion to his followers about the inability of man to serve two masters, God and Mammon, and urging them to labour in the Lord's field alone and in no other. He further informed four rebel slaves, Colonel Dove, Colonel Gardner, Colonel Duhaney and Colonel Thorp, that 'Free paper has not come. Free Paper will never come. We must write it in our own blood.'

It was nearly Christmas and Sharp's plan of campaign had spread throughout all the plantations like wildfire. An attorney named Grignon was one of the first to discover the rebellious determination of the slaves when his headman, Colonel Dove, refused to whip a slave woman Grignon caught taking cane off the plantation for her own use. Dove informed the attorney of the slaves' intention to cease work after Christmas, and then Grignon was driven off his own estate. Naturally Grignon did not take this too kindly, so determined to teach the slaves a lesson, he sent out the militia. But the slaves had already taken to the bush, and the horsemen found the estate village strangely deserted.

On Christmas Day, the only holiday of the year granted to all slaves, while most of them danced and drank themselves into a state of insensibility, Sharp and his lieutenants passed round the final instructions for the revolt. Knibb was still making a desperate last ditch effort to dissuade any members of his congregation from joining the rebels, but it was hopeless, the situation by now was out of control. On 27 December 50,000 slaves broke free and set about burning and wrecking the plantation properties. Kensington trash house was fired, and later in the day after the family had left, the great house was broken into and plundered. Gangs of slaves roamed the island drumming up support, and at Ramble two headmen lined up the slaves from the estate at the point of a musket and made them swear to kill the white men. But there was very little murdering done by the slaves, first because it had never been part of Sharp's original intention, his objective being the attainment of liberty in as peaceable a fashion as possible, and second because most of the whites had fled the estates to seek refuge in the nearby towns or garrison posts. Furthermore, the slaves were no fighters, as was well illustrated by the battle on the Montpelier Estate, where a small body of militiamen routed three or four hundred armed slaves. One of the rebels had foolishly fired the trash house before they advanced, and the light of the flames allowed the defending militia to pick off their targets at leisure. One soldier was killed and four wounded, but the slaves suffered heavy casualties. For not only were they hopeless tacticians, but they were inadequately armed, some having muskets, but most only possessing home-made pikes, rusty cutlasses and wooden clubs.

But they did have one advantage, the bush, into which they melted whenever they were outgunned or outnumbered, so that by 29 December most of the interior had been abandoned to the slaves. The whites, still dreading massacre, had besieged themselves into Montego Bay and Falmouth to await the arrival of the army. Tales of atrocities were beginning to circulate among the planters and their families, but they were strictly tales and not facts. There was one certified case of the rape of some women held prisoner by the rebels, but no more than twelve whites were killed during the rebellion, most of them on active service and only four of them while going about their business. Indeed in the early days of the troubles the most remarkable aspect was the humanity and concern shown by the slaves to their captives. On one estate, Ginger Hill, the slaves disarmed the overseer and made him sign away his authority, but he was escorted to the cottage of a free black nearby where he remained prisoner while the estate was fired. A Mrs Graham, who lived on a remote hillside plantation, assumed she was to be murdered when the rebels broke into her house, but they

The treadmill in a slave prison in Jamaica

An abolitionist tract

were only looking for firearms and she was left alive and unharmed. Nevertheless, the white planters had this fixed idea that all the slaves were murderous savage beasts, and they fled before them like frightened children. When Captain Williams of the Navy arrived in Montego Bay he found the inhabitants and the refugees panic-struck, and doubtless if the slaves had decided to fire the town they could have massacred thousands.

With the arrival of the Army and Navy the tables were immediately turned. Major General Sir Willoughby Cotton issued a proclamation at the beginning of January which officially denied that emancipation had been granted, and which offered free pardon to any rebel slave who surrendered. Immediate vengeance was promised on any who chose to hold out. Soldiers and militiamen were sent inland to regain possession and by 5 January most of the rebels had surrendered, and most of the planters were returning to their estates. But although peace was easily and quietly restored, the real blood-letting was only just about to begin. The slaves had burnt over 150 properties, worth over half a million pounds. They had lost at least four hundred of their number, though the official reports gave exactly half that total as an estimate. But because of their disrespectful attitude towards their masters' sacred properties, they were to lose another hundred of their ranks by summary execution, and countless more were to suffer severe floggings and imprisonment. And once again the planters blamed the missionaries. 'Shooting is too honourable a death for men whose conduct has occasioned so much bloodshed, and the loss of so much property,' ranted a Jamaican newspaper. 'There are many fine hanging woods in St James and Trelawny, and we do sincerely hope that the bodies of all the Methodist preachers who may be convicted of sedition may diversify the scene.'

William Knibb was persecuted, publicly humiliated, thrown into gaol, threatened with the death sentence and finally exiled to England. Daddy Sharp, accused of being the ringleader, was hanged in front of Falmouth courthouse, although the planters would have preferred to see him broken on the wheel and exhibited in the town square. Parties of militiamen rode round the island smashing the chapels, burning negroes' houses, and to add spice to the sport, shooting 'suspected' rebel slaves on sight. By February they had the situation totally under control, so martial law was suspended, but the trials of the rebels continued into April. Of the 634 slaves tried, 310 were executed, and 285 punished. This was the official retribution for the destruction of the plantations and the loss of fourteen free lives. It was impossible to assess the unofficial number of slave deaths.

William Knibb from a colour print by George Baxter

A baptismal ceremony in Jamaica from a colour print by George Baxter

The exile of Knibb and of another Methodist, Henry Whiteley, to England caused a great stir. Once again the public seemed more concerned with the fates of white missionaries in the Caribbean rather than with the intolerable existence of the slaves themselves. But whatever the root cause of their dismay the lectures delivered around Britain by Knibb and the publication of Whiteley's tract called *Three Months in Jamaica* which sold 20,000 copies in two weeks, soon refocused the attention of the people to the proper problem – the desperate need for immediate emancipation.

So battle was once more joined in Parliament, and once more it was an uphill struggle. Whatever the clamour of the populace was outside the doors of Westminster, inside the House preferred to continue its game of procrastination and deferment. The 1832 Abolition Bill was defeated by 136 to ninety-two, the Members of Parliament being more concerned in trying to define what the proper compensation to the planters should be, despite the very accurate criticism levelled by the anonymous author of *Letters to the More Influential Classes* that 'to the slave holder nothing is due, to the slave everything'. In 1833 no mention was made in the speech from the Throne at the opening of Parliament concerning the abolition of slavery at all, and Stanley, the new Colonial Secretary and future Prime Minister, declared himself to be unsympathetic towards the previous proposals for emancipation.

Public opinion was not deterred. Petitions flooded Parliament with almost a million and a half signatures, the largest single petition being signed by 187,000 women, all members of the Ladies' Anti-Slavery Society. A procession of clergymen from the Established Church and the Dissenting Ministeries marched on Downing Street to protest about the proposed compensation planned to alleviate the sufferings of the planters when their property was emancipated. To all the radicals within the movement this proposal seemed to be in direct conflict with the premise of the anti-slavery argument, namely that slavery was illegal. Compensation implied the acceptance of a legal basis to slavery. And the public were staunchly opposed to such a ridiculous and expensive hand-out.

By May 1833 the government could resist no longer and Stanley outlined his principles to the House. Any further attempt at amelioration was rejected and a system of compensatory apprenticeship was outlined to prevent the planters from suffering 'hardship through loss of labour'. This scheme was only another version of slavery, because it proposed that all slaves over six years old should continue working three-quarters of their time for their existing masters for a period of twelve years, and to further compensate for the loss of a quarter of the slaves' labour, the planters were to be loaned £15 million.

'It is quite clear,' said Stanley, 'that the repayment must be borne either by the produce of the negro, or by the revenue of this country. It cannot in justice be borne by the planter.'

Which meant that the slaves would have to 'buy' their freedom, as if by their unpaid labour they had not 'earned' it already.

Parliament, insensitive as ever to the injustice of these proposals, carried the resolutions by a comfortable majority, and James Stephen drafted the Bill in two and a half days, working over into a Sunday for only the second time in his life. The abolitionists won a minor victory by amending the apprenticeship period to six years, but suffered a major defeat when the loan of £15m was changed to a gift of £20m. Buxton had tried to press for immediate and unconditional emancipation, but this only started to reactivate the old debate about whether or not the black was fit for freedom, argued most notably by Robert Peel, who was 'worried' by the problem of amalgamating black and white, and 'concerned' about the negroes' 'aversion to hard labour'. Other supporters argued that the negro slaves would be less fit for liberty at the end of the apprenticeship period than they were before it, because they would slip into slothful and idle ways without the whip on their backs. Daniel O'Connell refuted all these nonsensical arguments with the statement that 'Men who can bear slavery most assuredly offer a very strong presumption that they can bear freedom'.

Even so, the majority of the members of Parliament nursed grave doubts about the possible repercussions of even this controlled emancipation, and expressed fears that when the Bill was enacted there would be a subsequent bloodbath in the colonies.

On 5 July 1833 the Bill for the Abolition of Slavery was finally introduced, and news was brought to the now dying Wilberforce of the great debate. Sadly he did not live to see the Bill enacted, for he died two days before that famous day. On 31 July it was passed and on 29 August it became law. Its opponents stood back and awaited the massacre. Once again they were to be proved criminally wrong in their assessment of the situation, for on the plantations the slaves simply danced and rejoiced. No blood was shed and no white man killed. And the next day the slaves resumed work on the plantations, now as 'apprentices' in a job with which they had become more than fully conversant.

The proclamation of the emancipation of the slaves, Spanish Town, Jamaica
1 August 1834

A cartoon ridiculing the reluctance of Britain to pay the West Indian planters the
£20 million Parliament had voted as compensation for the emancipation of the slaves

7. Aftermath

The Act of 1833 abolishing slavery within the British colonies opened the flood gates for another orgy of national self-congratulation, which was to last well into the following century. Parliament was particularly aglow with self-esteem, congratulating itself on its philanthropy and humanity when it should have been hiding its head in shame. For right up to the end Parliament refused to recognise the fact that slavery was both immoral and illegal, since the Abolition Act itself finally recognised the right of one man's legal ownership over another by granting compensation and by legalising the ridiculous system of apprenticeship which was only 'slavery in disguise'. The fact that the British public was prepared to pay twenty million pounds out of its pocket was evidence of its charity, however misguided, and its determination to be finally rid of the obnoxious system of slavery, but its motives were in direct contrast to those of Parliament, who felt honour bound to compensate the plantation owners purely for their loss of property. For the gift of these millions only further enriched families such as the Gladstones, the Pinneys and the Harewoods who had founded their fortunes initially on slaving. These absentee owners took enormous percentages of the gift before the actual plantation owners still working in the Caribbean ever received any of it, the Pinneys, for instance, deducting of the £145,000 granted to the planters of Nevis at least £32,000 by direct and indirect means. It was a very satisfactory conclusion indeed – for the creditors and plantation owners.

But while the rich families were getting rich satisfaction from the Abolition Act, the inadequate and indefensible system of 'apprenticeship' was already breaking down. Reports were reaching England that many of the slaves were actually worse off under the new scheme than they were before, so in 1836 a committee was set up to enquire into what the situation was actually like in the colonies. Joseph Sturge, yet another remarkably energetic abolitionist, was determined to acquire first-hand information, so he personally toured Martinique, Dominica, Antigua and Montserrat as well as the main islands and published his report as soon as he returned to England. It contained much evidence about the continuing abuses and punishments imposed on the 'apprentices', and proved that besides collecting their compensation most planters were simply ignoring the Act. Once again a furore was created

Thomas Clarkson addressing the members of the anti-slavery convention, held in London in June 1840

and Parliament was inundated with petitions, so that finally in 1838 a resolution was passed by three votes in favour of abolishing the system. But the man who passed it, Sir Eardley Wilmot, reneged on his promise to follow up his resolution when threatened by the government, expressing the feeble hope that the resolution would act as sufficient encouragement to bring an end to the system.

It was the colonies themselves who, realising their luck had run out, finally abolished apprenticeship, Antigua leading the way and Jamaica, predictable to the last, bringing up the rear. By August 1838 full freedom had been granted throughout the colonies, but the resultant celebrations were once more orderly and relatively sober, prompting the Bishop of Jamaica to remark that he had never seen such an 'impressive and affecting scene'. But it spelt the end for the West Indian empire and freedom for 700,000 blacks. Some stayed on the estates, but the majority drifted away to build a life of their own. So much for the predictions of there being a resultant 'grateful peasantry'. White labour was impossible to find, so the planters made desperate attempts to work the plantations with imported Indian labour, but the West Indian sugar trade was doomed, and its economy already crumbling. By 1836 it collapsed completely when the British preference on West Indian sugar was swept away on the tide of Free Trade, as Adam Smith had correctly predicted sixty years before. The Abolitionists' work was done. The day of liberation had arrived.

It is difficult to assess precisely what was the most influential factor that brought about the end to the most despicable chapter in British history. It certainly was not Parliament, although it enacted the bills that made the trade itself illegal and final emancipation a possibility. Parliament, because of the vested interests of many of its members and the inherent conservatism of both houses, actually protracted the struggle and never persuaded itself of the immorality of slavery. The Abolitionists who were members of Parliament most certainly fought an eloquent and energetic campaign at Westminster, but their final influence within Parliament was weakened by the refusal of many of the anti-slaving members to disassociate themselves completely from the West Indian influence and by their inability to understand the needs of the people they were earnestly trying to emancipate and 'improve'. Their best work was done outside the House, and nothing can minimise the achievement of those tireless crusaders who toured Britain and the Caribbean in search of the evidence that they knew would inevitably destroy the iniquitous system of slavery. Their fearless campaigning in the field united public opinion, and in those days of pre-reformed Parliament, public opinion could often have great effect. It is more or less irrelevant to criticise the motives of some of the Abolitionists. To us they may have seemed unduly concerned with 'Christianising' the blacks before granting them full emancipation, but to their opponents at that time, even this mild policy was dangerously radical. They were brave men and women, and without their integrity and energetic endeavours, Parliament would never even have been aware of the injustices and barbarities practised under the slave system.

The planters are an even easier target, and with a few notable exceptions, they richly deserved the vituperation later bestowed upon them. They were mostly vicious, selfish, ignorant and thoughtless masters, but there is some slight justification for the Claphamites' desire to exonerate them of blame, because if there had been no slave trade, and no slave system, there would have been no brutal plantation owners. However, it is impossible finally to vindicate unspeakable brutality, and the fact that there were some notably humane, philanthropic, and popular planters is enough to condemn the rest of them to a legacy of notoriety. Perhaps the real enemy of slavery was slavery itself, for it finally collapsed only when it was unworkable economically. A sense of morality, and remarkable eloquence are notable attributes, but neither are sufficient to destroy anything economically stable.

The campaign against slavery produced many extraordinary men and invented a method of protest that set the blueprint for modern civil resistance. It was energetic, fearless and honest, which is more than can be said of Parliament's role in the conflict. But unfortunately, the abolition of slavery as we know now, in no way brought an end to racial conflict, nor did the fight to achieve emancipation help towards a better understanding of the black. For once slavery had been accepted both as an economic and as a social custom the black was regarded increasingly as an inferior. This belief started on the coast of Africa as the white overseers and traders loaded the hundreds of blacks into the holds of the slave ships, and was fostered on the plantations. Blackness became synonomous with enslavement. Before the end of the sixteenth century, there is practically no literary or artistic reference to suggest that the black was considered inferior, but once slave trading became a widely practised custom in the European countries, references start appearing about the 'thick lipp'd slave' and suggesting the total inferiority of the negro race. From there on the negro became a despised and feared savage, an unintelligent brute unworthy of any human rights, and deserving only to be mocked and disparaged. White came to mean purity, and black came to mean evil.

Africa today still bears the marks that slavery cut into her land. The political map of her West Coast was determined during the height of the slave trade, when the massive fortresses and slaving ports dominated the coastline, for subsequently these became the focal points of each region, and dependant colonies grew up around them. As has been seen, it suffered massive depopulation as a result of the slave transportations, losing the prime of its man and womanhood to the sugar colonies or to early graves in the Atlantic. It indulged in the disreputable art of inter-tribal warfare which further decimated its dwindling population, and by constant exposure to the ways of the white rulers it learnt about corruption and materialistic greed. Even the spread of Christianity gave little benefit to the African, for it simply protracted the myth of white superiority by constantly casting the negro in the role of pupil. Slavery brutalised the whole continent, at the same time removing any national incentive, for to the inhabitants there seemed little point in planning anything for the future when tomorrow they could either be kidnapped or murdered. The best of their craftsmen were stolen from them, their native culture withered and died, and even the fabric of the family unit was destroyed. By the time the last slave ships left its shores for the Caribbean, Africa was a dark and terrible place.

Slavery bred racialism and colour prejudice, and we have it to thank for these twin shadows which fall over our modern civilisation. It brought to America as a work force a people who now threaten revolution if they are not granted the same rights and opportunities enjoyed there by the white population. America has one of the largest negro populations in the world, second only to Nigeria, but since emancipation successive white governments have steadfastly refused to grant equality, due solely to the racialist fear that the blacks are not fit for equality. Once they were not fit for freedom. Now they are being made to fight for equal citizenship. And however ill-founded these fears have been proved to be, the bigotry is so deep rooted that many people earnestly believe the black to be naturally inferior mentally and physically to the white.

It has been proved repeatedly that in no way is the intellect of the negro inferior to that of the white man but factual evidence is no match for entrenched bigotry. Even more ridiculous now is the fact that it has become politically taboo to discuss whether any differences do indeed exist between the two races, when the experts acknowledge such to be the case, although we may constantly refer to the differences between nations, and either judge or condemn foreigners on these discrepancies. The experts inform us that there are marked metaphysical differences between black and white, whether racially or culturally derived, the black possessing an excellence in memory and intuition, and a wholesale difference in perception, in contrast to the white reliance on pragmatism and objective judgment. But western society has become so guilt ridden about the colour question that discussion on this subject is often outlawed since it seems to suggest criticism.

Yet nowadays, if our society is to be able to deal with the modern multi-racial problems, it is vital that we should try and understand each other better, so this ostrich-like behaviour will not help to solve anything. The French have made the most successful effort at integration by accepting the basic differences, calling it simply 'négritude'. They realise the negro often bases his actions on intuition rather than logic, and accept that he 'works to live' rather than believing in the guilty white ethic of being 'alive to work'. But elsewhere few people have so successfully bridged this philosphical gap, and panic struck, or fearful of a bloody tomorrow they continue to refuse equality and integration to their brothers. No better example of this can be found than South Africa, whose founders trekked away in disgust from Cape Colony after emancipation in 1835 because they found it intolerable that they should be expected to share equal footing with the heathen black, and in order to establish their own colonies where 'there shall be no equality between black and white in Church and State.'

In England today we are suffering from an increase in racial tension, and if we listen carefully to our own national conversation we can hear the repetition of many of the old arguments much despised by the fighters of slavery back in the eighteenth century. Whatever we think of the complexion of our modern society, the revival of ignorant fears and prejudices will do little to change or improve it. This country was the premier slaver in Europe, fattening its treasury and financing its all-important Industrial Revolution on the proceeds of a trade in human beings. The fact that many of us live so comfortably and securely only 140 years after its abolition should serve to remind us that the prosperity of this country in modern times was founded on the most notorious trade in history and this should give us sufficient incentive to try and repay some of this debt by moving at least towards a better understanding of our fellow men.

Acknowledgment is due to the following for permission to reproduce illustrations on the following pages:

End-papers: National Maritime Museum; Frontispiece: from 'A Description of the Coast of Guinea' by William Bosman (1721); Page 6, Wedgwood & Sons Ltd; 9, Wilberforce House Museum; 10, (above) from 'Cardiphonia' by John Newton, (below) Liverpool Packet No. 5 Scouse Press © Fritz Spiegl; 15, Ikon/ by courtesy of Lord Harlech; 16, (above) J. Allan Cash, (below) Peter Fraenkel; 17, from 'A Description of the Coast of Guinea' by William Bosman; 18, Fotomas Index; 19, from C. D. Wadstrom's 'Essay on Colonisation' (1794); 21, (above) United Society for the Propagation of the Gospel/Ikon, (below) Radio Times Hulton Picture Library; 22–3, Wilberforce House Museum; 24, (above) Fotomas, (below) Wilberforce House Museum; 28, (above) from C. D. Wadstrom's 'Essay on Colonisation' (1794), (below) Mary Evans Picture Library; 29, National Maritime Museum; 32–3, Liverpool Packet No. 5; 34–5, (left) Werner Forman Archive/Museum für Völkerkunde, Berlin-Dahlem, (right) Werner Forman Archive/British Museum; 36, Werner Forman Archive; 38–9, from T. Edward Bowdich's 'Mission to Ashantee' (1819); 41, Fotomas; 42, Dr. Johnson's House; 44, Wilberforce House Museum; 46–7, National Portrait Gallery; 50, Diana Phillips; 51, Wilberforce House Museum; 54, (above) from 'Histoire des Iles Antilles', (below) Roger Viollet; 55, (above) Mansell Collection, (below) Anne Bolt; 56, from Robert Bridgen's 'West India Sketches' (c.1836)/Royal Commonwealth Society; 57, (above) Mansell Collection, (below) Mary Evans Picture Library; 58, Wilberforce House Museum; 61, Ikon/from Dalzel's 'History of Dahomey' (1793); 65, National Portrait Gallery; 66, National Portrait Gallery; 70, from C. D. Wadstrom's 'Essay on Colonisation' (1794); 73, (above) Radio Times Hulton Picture Library, (below) from C. D. Wadstrom's 'Essay on Colonisation' (1794); 77, (above) Mary Evans Picture Library, (below) Wilberforce House Museum; 78, Wilberforce House Museum; 82–3, from Captain Crow's 'Memoirs' (1830); 86–7, National Portrait Gallery; 90, Ikon/ from Equiano's 'Travels'; 91, Royal Albert Memorial Museum, Exeter; 92, National Portrait Gallery; 95, Roger Viollet; 97, Fotomas; 101, National Portrait Gallery; 103, British Museum; 105, Ikon; 106, (above) from 'A History of Jamaica' by Edward Long (1774), (below left) Anne Bolt, (below right) Jamaica Tourist Board; 107, Jamaica Tourist Board; 108, Anne Bolt; 111, (above) Fotomas, (below) from Clarkson's 'History of the Abolition of the African Slave Trade' (1808); 115, Wilberforce House Museum; 116, Royal Commonwealth Society/from Bridgen's 'West India Sketches'; 120, from 'The Anti-Slavery Record', 1835/Fotomas; 121, from Bryan Edwards' 'History of the British Colonies in the West Indies' (1801); 129, (above) Mary Evans Picture Library, (below) Royal Commonwealth Society; 131, Victoria and Albert Museum; 134, (above) Royal Commonwealth Society/from 'Jamaica' by James M. Philippo (1843), (below) Mansell Collection; 136–7, National Portrait Gallery.

143

ACKNOWLEDGMENTS

The television series on which this book is based was largely researched by the use of contemporary writings, diaries, letters, essays, pamphlets, sermons, court records and parliamentary debates.

However, the authors would also like to acknowledge, and to recommend for further reading, the following published works:

COUPLAND, Sir Reginald   *The British Anti-Slavery Movement*   F. Cass, 2nd edn. 1964.

COUPLAND, Sir Reginald   *Wilberforce: a narrative*   Clarendon Press, 2nd edn. 1945.

CROW, H.   *The memoirs of Harriet Crow*   F. Cass, reprint of 1830 edition 1970.

DAVIDSON, B.   *Africa: history of a continent*   Spring Books, rev. edn. 1972.

DAVIDSON, B.   *Black mother*   Gollancz, 1961.

EHRMAN, J.   *The younger Pitt*   Constable, 1969.

ELMES, J.   *Thomas Clarkson: his life and labours*   London, 1854.

EQUIANO, O.   *Travels*   edited by P. Edwards. Heinemann, 1970.

FORDE, D. ed.   *Efik traders of old Calabar, containing the diary of Antera Duke*   Dawsons of Pall Mall, 1968.

FURNEAUX, R.   *William Wilberforce*   H. Hamilton, 1974.

GRATUS, J.   *The great white lie: slavery emancipation and changing racial attitudes*   Hutchinson, 1972.

GRIGGS, E. L.   *Thomas Clarkson: the friend of slaves*   Allen and Unwin, 1936.

HAMPSHIRE, C.   *The British in the Caribbean*   Weidenfeld and Nicolson, 1972.

HOARE, P.   *The memoirs of Granville Sharp*   London, 1820.

LASCELLES, E. C. P.   *Granville Sharp and the freedom of the slaves in England*   Humphrey Milford, 1928.

MACKENZIE-GRIEVE, A.   *The last years of the English slave trade, Liverpool, 1750–1807*   F. Cass, 1968.

MANNIX, D. P.   *Black cargoes: a history of the Atlantic slave trade, 1518–1865*   Longmans, 1963.

NEWTON, J.   *The journal of a slave trader* edited by B. Martin and M. Spurrell. Epworth Press, 1962.

NUGENT, Lady Maria   *Journal* edited by F. Cundall. Kingston: Institute of Jamaica, 3rd edn. 1939.

POPE-HENNESSY, J.   *The sins of the fathers: a study of the Atlantic slave traders, 1441–1807*   Weidenfeld and Nicolson, 1967.

RANSFORD, O.   *The slave trade*   J. Murray, 1971.

REID, L.   *Charles James Fox*   Longmans, 1969.

WALVIN, J.   *Black and white: the negro and English society, 1555–1945*   Allen Lane, 1973.

WEBSTER, J. B. and BOAHEN, A. A.   *Revolutionary years: West Africa since 1800*   Longman, 1970.

WILLIAMS, E. E.   *Capitalism and slavery*   Deutsch, 1964.

WRIGHT, P.   *Knibb the Notorious: slaves' missionary, 1803–45*   Sidgwick and Jackson, 1973.